Praise for SAVING FACE

"I have known Vicki for 20+ years, working together at different beauty salons. She does not age ... fabulous for 76 years young. Her radiant skin is youthful and always glowing. I always ask her what is her secret. Seeing her skin up close, while doing her eyebrows and make up, I see everything, she is practically flawless.

Her book called *Saving Face* is chalked full of great beauty tips and secrets to looking and feeling great as you age."

–Rosett Schoenwald, Rosett Coosmetics, Cosmetician

"I've known Vicki Le Mere since 1984 when she became a Buddhist in our district, working for world peace. Although she was 38 at the time and had three children, she looked like she had just graduated from college. She had suffered through two abusive marriages and her youngest daughter had special needs, I watched the light in her life grow and grow through her spiritual practice and no one could ever guess her age. She has actually grown younger looking in these past 37 years and most importantly, she has transformed her life. Her book is a wonderful journey through her life and her secrets to beauty and spiritual fulfillment."

–Dr. Clinton Jones: Chiropractor, NFL alumni, College Football
Hall of Fame Inductee and Buddhist District Leader

"I have known Vicki Le Mere for over 10 years as a friend, exercise partner and confidant about all things skin and beauty. Her knowledge has been a constant source of amazement to me, and the story of her life as related to me over the years is an incredible adventure. Now she has bravely shared all that in her new book *Saving Face,* in which she reveals not only her valuable beauty tips but the fascinating, sometimes harrowing, journey of her life toward peace and fulfillment. Vicki is a beautiful woman with a beautiful soul with so much to offer to her readers.

–Pamela De Almeida, cellist New West Symphony,
California Philharmonic, Moorpark College (Principal),
Desert Symphony, Thousand Oaks Philharmonic

Saving Face

A Great-Grandmother Shares Her Life-Long Secrets
to Beauty and Happiness

Saving Face

VICKI LE MERE

Published by Buddha Baby Books

ISBN (paperback): 979-8-88796-923-7
ISBN (ebook): 979-8-88796-924-4

Book design by Christy Day, Constellation Book Services

Printed in the United States of America

I dedicate this book to my wonderful children whom I love so dearly: Nicky, Todd, Aviva. And to my wonderful grandchildren: Ashley, Brittney, Bodhi, Finley. And to my precious great grand-children; Destiny, Terra, and Wolf.

I also dedicate this book to my dearest friend and confidant, Joyce whom I lost ten years ago. My darling Joyce you always inspired me to write and you loved my writing. I will never forget your encouraging words and your love.

Contents

Introduction

My book is about finding inner happiness and outer ageless beauty. I will take you on the journey of my life from age fourteen to seventy-five. I will tell you how I navigated through the trials and tribulations of my life, and ended up finding a way to be happy and look great at every age. In these pages, I will share with you twenty-five key secrets and tips to ageless beauty. One of the things I never wanted to do was have plastic surgery. I found ways to avoid doing that and learned many secrets to eternal beauty. You will see that I did not have an easy life; however, I finally learned how to have a happy life, full of joy. I would like to share with you all of the things I have learned about going from being a victim to a victor. I would like to help women and men, as well, to age gracefully so they can be their most beautiful selves. Being happy is not only important in life; it is your right. I will show you how I learned to develop the kind of happiness that no situation or person could take away from me. Looking good is great, but if you do not feel great inside it shows on your face and accelerates the aging process.

I started working as a model at fifteen-years-old. Because I was in the beauty business, I started reading and studying everything I could get my hands on that involved skin care and makeup. Over the years, I learned a lot and put into practice many tips and secrets you will find in my book. These routines and practices have helped me to look ten to fifteen years younger than my age for most of my life, and today as well. My routine is very simple and does not involve many expensive skin care products.

When it comes to the face, I have a lot of experience and knowledge that I have gleaned over the years. When it comes to inner happiness, I have learned many things that I would like to share with you. The face reflects your inner feelings. In other words, as the famous quote from Dorian Gray says, "If you do not like the image in the mirror, do not break the Looking Glass." As a teenager, people would tell me how cute, beautiful or gorgeous I was, but I did not believe them. I did not feel good or beautiful on the inside. Due to my abusive childhood and destructive relationships, I was a mess! I had to learn how to get rid of my victim mentality so that I could not only look good, but more importantly, feel good.

One of the things I thought about as a teenager was how I could start then to save my face from aging. I guess that was a funny thing for a teenager to be thinking about. However, at sixteen, when everything is all about your face and the way you look, that was what I thought was important.

I worked as a model for fifteen years and learned many

things about inner and outer beauty. The journey to *Saving Face* has brought me to this present moment.

I would like to share a story with you:

The other day I had a massage and I asked the woman how old she thought I was. She said she thought I was forty-five. I am seventy-five! That was funny to me. I figured it was time for me to share my secrets. Nobody wants to get old and, for sure, nobody wants to look old. Aging is part of life, but let us do it gracefully and without plastic surgery, if possible. In this book I will share many secrets and tips that worked for me and I believe will work for you, as well.

Do you not want to look your very best at every age? This book will help you to achieve that goal. It does not matter what age you are. Start now and the benefits will follow. I want you to have the happiest, most fulfilling life possible and to be your most beautiful self. This book will:

- Teach you ways to save your face
- Make you laugh and make you cry
- Teach you how to change sadness into happiness
- Make you feel happy
- Give you twenty-five beauty secrets of a (not my words) gorgeous great grandma

PART ONE

The Journey

CHAPTER 1

Abusive Childhood

My mother told me that I was singing and dancing before I could walk or talk. I would entertain my relatives at our Sunday get-togethers. I was about three years old at the time, and I looked like a cute little Shirley Temple. I had blonde ringlets and I would sing the latest songs from the radio. However, I would sing the wrong words and people would just fall down laughing. In one song I used sing it was supposed to be "lover's device" and I would sing "livers device" because that is how my young ears interpreted it from the radio. My mother used to cook liver all the time and make us eat it. I guess that is where I learned the word. At that age, I knew a lot more about livers than I did about lovers. These experiences at a very young age are what hooked me on singing and doing comedy. My aunts and uncles would reward me with quarters, so I made money entertaining. Ha ha. I was the life of the party and I enjoyed all the attention I received as a little girl.

My mother and father fought a lot, and my father was an abusive alcoholic. Of course, I did not understand this at the time, as I was only a little girl. When you grow up in a dysfunctional family, you do not know that you are growing up in a dysfunctional family because that is all you know. I am sure my mother was upset and angry a lot because my father abused her, too. I think she took it out on us. I have a sister who is two years older than I am who also abused me while we were growing up. I was spanked a lot, and sometimes hit with a wooden spoon. I do not know if she was spanked as much as I was, but I doubt it. Despite suffering abuse from both of my parents, I was a happy child by nature.

Besides spanking me, my mother used to do other abusive things to me. I did not like to eat hardly anything that I can remember. I liked breakfast and I liked Libby's pork and beans with buttered toast. Sometimes, on Friday nights we would make tomato soup and have it with fresh bread from the bakery. I really liked that. I mostly hated dinners when I was young. My mother used to make many gross things every night like: lima beans, Brussels sprouts, parsnips, and mashed potatoes. I hated all of them, especially mashed potatoes. I would sit there with my dinner in front of me and not eat it. I would try to feed it to the dog, but he did not want it either. Then I would try to stuff it into my pockets or drop it behind the refrigerator. I would do anything to get rid of the food and not have to eat it. Sometimes I would get away with it and sometimes I would not, but one thing for sure; I was not going to eat that food. It made me want to barf. After about an hour, they would try to force feed me the cold potatoes by shoving them down my throat. I would gag on them. Then they would end up putting me in the basement with the dog and lock the door. I was locked in a dirty, musty smelling old basement with a dirty, smelly, old dog. The poor old dog would be let out to poop and he would get covered in snow and come back wet when they let him back in so he smelled like a dirty wet dog. No one ever bathed him. He was abused, as well. I remember my mother letting him in the front door and kicking him into the basement.

There were cobwebs everywhere in that basement. They were hanging from the rafters, and I am sure there were lots of spiders. Add to that the pungent smell of dog poop, and you get a picture of how wrong this was. The worst thing they would do is turn out the light so it would be pitch black. I was scared, and they would leave me there for what seemed like hours. That was child abuse. Actually, it never came to me as being child abuse until just recently. I thought about it and now I can say for sure that that was child abuse.

It totally got worse when I was eight-and-a-half-years old. That is when my baby sister Janet was born. Do not get me wrong, I was happy about having a baby sister. The problem was that I had contracted whooping cough and I gave it to the newborn baby. My parents had never had me vaccinated for this disease. They blamed me for giving it to the baby, and they were very angry with me all the time. In order to save the baby's life, they had to stay up all night and take turns holding her upside down every time she coughed. Moreover, they let me know it was my fault. I would be crying and coughing and whooping until I threw up, and they would yell at me angrily, "Go clean it up!" Not only had I lost all the attention of being the baby in the family, now I was the villain of the family. Is it any wonder that I learned to be a victim at a very young age?

CHAPTER 2

Summers at the Lake With Grandparents and My First Love

When I think about the best times I ever had as a child, they were the summers I spent at the lake with my grandmother and grandfather. Every summer, my mother would dump me off there. At first I hated it. I was around nine years old at that time and there was nothing to do. My grandmother was sweet and kind to me, but I think she sensed my boredom. I would make her laugh a lot, and I guess that was my second experience at doing stand-up comedy. Life at the lake was rough. You might say we were roughing it. We had no indoor bathrooms, no electricity and of course, no TVs. We would listen to the radio.

My grandmother lived year-round in a beach community called Grand Marais, Manitoba on Lake Winnipeg. She had many interesting hobbies; she was always working on something. She made sun hats for the local what she called "Indian children" and beautiful quilts for her family. She was always sewing something. My grandmother was a fisher woman, as well. She would put her nets in every night with the help of the locals, whom she called "the half-breeds." A half-breed was someone who was half American Indian and half English or French. My grandmother on my father's side was half-French and half-American Indian. I guess that made me some sort of half-breed, too. When my grandmother would bring in her nets the next day, we would have barrels of fish. Therefore, of course, that is mostly what we had for dinner. I hated it. My grandmother would overcook it and it was powdery and dry with little bones in it. I would choke on the bones, all the time. At that moment, I swore when I was grown up that I would never eat fish for the rest of my life.

My grandfather, whom we were told to call Tom, was a sweet, kind old man. He had a big bushy mustache, and when I wanted to kiss him, I would lift up his mustache so it would not prickle me. He used to call me his "sweet wee soul." He was crippled and walked with two canes. Apparently, years before he had jumped off a train to avoid being involved in a train wreck that had killed nearly everyone on board. He was sent to the morgue for dead, but when they went to pull the blanket up over his head, someone saw him blink his eyes and they realized he was still alive. He had broken multiple bones in his feet and legs.

Tom was the local magistrate. Glass doors separated his office from the rest of the house. Many times, I saw the local RCMP (Royal Canadian Mounted Police) officers bringing in criminals to pay fines or possibly be put in handcuffs and taken off to jail.

I have fond memories of my grandfather. I remember him pulling out a special box of tobacco from a hidden spot. I am sure my grandmother did not want him smoking so much. It never bothered me. I thought it smelled sweet and wonderful. With his old crippled fingers, he would perch the box on his lap and pinch out just the right amount of tobacco. Then he would place that snatch into the bowl of one of his favorite pipes. Gently, he would press the tobacco into the bowl with just the right amount of pressure. When he had it perfectly packed, he would reach for his box of matches and strike one on the side of the box. You could see his joy as he lit the bowl and inhaled his first puff. I have never liked the smell of cigarette smoke, but this was heavenly.

My grandfather also smoked cigarettes, which he would roll himself with those old crippled fingers. He was artful at it, though; always getting the perfect amount of tobacco and rolling a perfect cigarette. You would think with all that smoking, he would have died young, but he lived well into his nineties.

Knowing that I was incredibly bored, my grandmother introduced me to a nearby family who had two boys and a girl, around my age. They were the Warner family. The boys were one and two years older than I was, and Bonnie, the daughter, was a year younger than I was. I have to say, my interest was mostly in Ronnie, the second youngest brother. I hung out with Bonnie hoping to see Ronnie. I was twelve going on fifteen, if you know what I mean. This is when the fun began.

The family seemed rather well off. They had a beautiful summer home overlooking the lake with probably six to seven bedrooms. Mr. Warner was a rugged, handsome and athletic-looking man. Mrs. Warner was older-looking and rather stout. In the summer, it was customary for the children to stay at the lake for the summer with their mothers, or in my case, grandmother, while the fathers worked in the city of Winnipeg. The fathers would always come out for the weekends and sometimes stay an extra day or two. They would take a few weeks off work in the summer to spend more time with their families at the lake.

Mr. Warner arrived one weekend with a brand new Cadillac convertible. I will never forget how beautiful it was. It was two-toned pink; long and luxurious. The Warners also had a speedboat with all the accessories; skies, surfboards, etc. We would spend a lot of time at the nearby beach. The boys loved to drive the family boat, and they would always pull us girls behind on either the surfboard or the skis. What fun we had. One day, I was in the boat with my sister and my love interest, Ronnie. He was driving the boat. He was going so fast that I told my sister if he went any faster, my top would come off. She told him what I said and he immediately pushed as hard as he could on the throttle, which was already at the max. That was a good sign for me.

It meant that he liked me; or it could have been that he just wanted to see me without my top on. I guess I was getting somewhat cute.

In the nighttime, we would play a game that was kind of like hide-and-go-seek but we called it "releavo." The person who was "it" would have to hide their eyes while the rest all of us went off into various areas. Many of the kids would be in couples, and I was fortunate enough to be with Ronnie on one of these occasions. The poor person that was "it" never got to find anyone, because we had no intention of being found. Some of the couples would make out in the bushes and some would just talk and have friendly exchanges. One night, Ronnie walked me home after our game. He kissed me at the back door. I was over the moon and I guess I told my grandmother about it because the next day, my grandfather was joking around and said that he almost slipped on all the slobber by the back door. My secret was out. That was my first kiss and I was smitten.

CHAPTER 3

Beauty and Abuse

Later that summer, I entered a bathing beauty contest. You had to walk on a runway in a bathing suit and impress the judges. They were from the local beach council. I was fourteen-years-old and I had a hot body for my age. I added a little padding here and a little pinch in there, and voila! It was so much fun. I did not really think I was that good looking because I had low self-esteem. Having grown up in an abusive family, even though people would tell me how cute I was, I did not believe them. However, I won the contest and I was very excited. My prize was a blue train case. It could be used for makeup or as an overnight case. I treasured that case for many years and always remembered that this was the beginning of my journey to beauty and happiness.

My father was an alcoholic. He would abuse my mother and sometimes hit her. As a little girl, I was very afraid for my mother, my sister and me. My father had a violent temper and sometimes he would knock us around the room. It felt like I was bouncing off the walls. Other times, he would take us upstairs to the bedroom where he would pull off his

16

belt. He would make a snapping noise with it to scare us, and then he would strike us with the belt several times. He only did one of us at a time, so I am not sure if my sister got the belt as many times as I did. It is quite possible that I was the more defiant one and therefore got more spankings than my sister did. My sister grew up hating my father and didn't talk to him for decades.

Although my father was abusive to us, as I got older I understood why. He had had a terrible childhood. He told me about how the nuns abused him when he was a little boy. His mother, who was half-French and half-American Indian, left his father because he was an alcoholic and abusive. She had seven children with him. After she left him, she had no way to care for her children, so she put them in various places; some with foster parents and some into the monastery with the nuns. As she was Catholic, this was an easy decision. My father told me about the abuse he received while with the nuns. He said that the nuns would hold the small children's heads under water in the bathtub to punish them, and they would put wet underwear on them and smack them with a paddle.

My father ran away and was captured and put into a foster home. He said that was just as bad as the monastery, and they made him eat fish heads every night. The foster kids had no toys, and were only allowed to play with sticks and tin cans. My father ran away from this situation, as well. At nine-years-old, he was homeless, living on the street selling newspapers. He never had any formal education; maybe only grades one and two. He had so little love as a child; it's hard to believe that he would even know how to love as a parent.

The reason I tell this story is that I saw a piece on *60 Minutes* about finding the unknown graves of many Indian children in Canada. Apparently, there was a period in time in Canada when the government took the American Indian children away from their parents, as they wanted to educate them and they put them in the Catholic boarding schools with the nuns. One of the older American Indian women interviewed said, "I am mean and I am angry for the way I was abused as a child." These stories help me understand why my father was so abusive because of his childhood.

When I was fifteen-years-old I won a contest for the Hudson Bay Company, the largest department store in Canada. There were hundreds of girls trying out, and those chosen got to model in a weeklong fashion show and contest. Fifteen girls would make it to be in the fashion show. After modeling for a week in the fashion show, votes would be counted and a winner would be crowned the new "Teen Queen" for that season. I made it into the fashion show along with fourteen other girls.

While shopping in the store, people would come by and see the fashion show. Afterwards they could vote for their favorite model. The votes were tallied at the end of two weeks, and surprise, surprise, I WON! I was so excited! My life was going in the direction I had secretly hoped it would. The prizes included a complete wardrobe and a modeling career for the Hudson Bay Company. I would be doing print work for their newspaper ads and making appearances in the store for special events. I also would be modeling in all of their adult fashion shows. I would have to say, this felt like the first real accomplishment of my life. I was thrilled!

After a year as teen queen, I relinquished my crown. The next set of teen hopefuls were chosen and I prepared to be the commentator for their show. The fashions were lovely and I wrote descriptions for each of the outfits. In the meantime, I continued my modeling career. I did fashion shows on the runway and appeared in the newspaper almost every night. I loved all the attention and it made me feel special, even though inside I thought I was not. Beauty had become an important part of my life. Even with all the accolades, I felt empty inside.

CHAPTER 4

Teen Pregnancy
Teen Marriage
(Beauty Tips 1, 2, & 3)

My dreams and aspirations came to a screeching halt at sixteen-and-a-half-years-old when I got pregnant. My mother wanted me to get married quickly, "before the neighbors found out." Brad, the person I married, was controlling and physically abusive to me. He would walk in the front door and punch me in the face. I never knew what I had done wrong, but it did not matter because he would not talk to me, anyway. We would sometimes go to the lake where his parents had a fishing resort. I remember one time I had to go to the bathroom and he would not stop to let me go. It was a three-hour drive. Another time he pushed me out of a moving car. And on and on. I was scared and miserable. On a cold and rainy day, I walked to the edge of a cliff and looked down at the waves crashing on the rocks below. I thought to myself that I could just let myself fall off and end the misery for me and my unborn child. I quickly whisked away that thought, as I did not want to hurt my family any more. I never told anyone in my family what was going on. I really felt like I deserved to be punished because I had been a bad girl and gotten myself pregnant. My mother always used to say that in one foolish moment you can ruin your whole life. I believed her now, and I pulled the curtain down on my life.

I had turned turned seventeen by the time by the time I delivered my sweet baby girl, Sherry. She was adorable but a real handful. I knew nothing about being a mother, so I depended on my mother to tell me what to do. I was breastfeeding, and one day I mixed her cereal with whole milk, not realizing it was too harsh for her baby stomach. Sherry projectile vomited across the room several times. I was so scared. I called the pediatrician and he told me I had to pump my own milk because cow's milk was not good for the new baby. I painfully pumped enough milk to make her cereal and was about to feed her when Brad walked in and said "out." I could not get out fast enough, and with one fell swoop, he smashed the bowl and its contents against the wall. He was always like that and I would start shaking twenty minutes before I knew he was coming home. I lived in terror.

At eighteen-years-old I had my second child, a sweet baby boy we named Tommy after my grandfather. He was so good; he never cried and I would have to wake him up to feed him. He would sleep for over four hours between feedings. The abuse got worse. One day Brad knocked me down the stairs. I have back issues to this day because of that. People asked me, "Why didn't you call the police?" To tell you the truth, I thought this was normal. It is what my mother went through, and I thought it was just what I had to go through. I think the straw that broke the camel's back happened one day when I left Brad babysitting so that I could get some groceries. When I came back, he had let Tommy, our toddler son, color all over the walls. I was nagging at him about it and he picked up the kitchen chair he was sitting on and hit me in the face with it. The steel disc on the bottom caught me beside my eye. The doctor said a few more inches and I could have permanently lost my sight in that eye. Luckily, a few stitches fixed it up. At that moment, I knew I had had it. The nightmare was over. That was the last time he would ever lay a hand on me. I was done!

I always maintained my dreams of returning to modeling in the back of my mind during those nightmare years. I started to think a lot about beauty and aging. I wanted my face to look very good when I got older. I started studying older women wherever I would go. I would look at them in the malls, the banks, the grocery stores and study the lines on their faces. What was the first area to go? Aha! It was the eyes, and then the neck.

When I was nineteen, I went out and found the best eye cream I could buy. Aging was not going to happen to me. I began using it every night, and to this day I put eye cream on every night.

Beauty Tip #1— Use eye cream every night. Start whatever age you're at and never stop.

I continued to study every article I could get my hands on about skin care and aging. Why had no one written a book about this stuff? I had to rely on magazines like *Vogue, Cosmopolitan*, and *Glamour* etc. I learned that you have elastic tissue under the surface of your skin. It is what gives your skin its youthful appearance. Wow, this was huge! So if I handled my skin with care, I could retain my elasticity. Done!

Beauty Tip #2—Never pull the skin around your eyes. You will break the elastic tissue that keeps the skin young. Once it's broken, it doesn't come back. Be careful with the skin all over your face but especially around the eyes.

I read an article in one of my magazines about the importance of doing facial exercises. Have you ever noticed that men do not show age on their necks the same way women do? That is because they shave every day. Without being aware of it, men do their facial exercises every day for their neck and lower face while shaving. In addition, they are removing a layer of skin, something that women are not doing every day.

Beauty Tip #3—Do facial exercises like men do when they are shaving. Pretend you are shaving without a blade. Also say the "A E I O U's". Exaggerate these vowels with extreme expressions on your face, out loud.

CHAPTER 5

Back to Modeling
(Beauty Tips 4, 5 and 6)

Back to my journey, I ended my abusive marriage after five years. I was broke, alone and in despair. However, I never stopped putting on that eye cream every night and doing my facial exercises.

A wonderful aunt of mine, who was a model, helped me get my own apartment and get on my feet again. She took me downtown to one of the clothing manufacturers, where I secured a job as a house model and secretary. As a house model, I would show the lines of clothing to various buyers, from department stores and individual stores. I was so happy. I was starting a new life. I had a job and my own place. I continued to care for my face to the best of my ability, keeping in mind my intention to look ten years younger than my age as I got older.

Beauty tip # 4—Set intentions for yourself!
I always intended to look a lot younger
than my age as I got older.

I was not much of a secretary, so I lost that part of my job after about one year, but I continued to be the house model for Fashion Ease whenever they needed me. It was not enough work for me to live on, so I began to work for a company called Holiday Magic cosmetics. The line had cosmetics and skin care products. I got my little case and I started selling to my friends. I would show them the line of products and let them try them. Taking orders was very exciting; it was a new little business for me. I loved to play with make-up, so it was perfect for me.

I learned the importance of not removing your makeup with soap. My studies had revealed that soap is drying and aging for the skin. I stopped using soap on my face. I have never used soap on my face to this day.

Beauty Tip # 5—Never use soap on your face,
it is drying and aging. Use cleansing cream and
wash it off with a warm washcloth.

Beauty Tip # 6—Put on your face cream and eye cream while your face is still wet. This locks in the moisture and enhances the effects of your beauty treatment.

2nd Marriage Birth of My Brain Damaged Daughter
(Beauty Tip 7)

I remember when I was a little girl I always wanted to look older. When I was twelve-years-old, I would go to the five-and-dime store and purchase mascara. I bought Maybelline cake mascara with a little brush. Every time I would get some mascara or lipstick, my parents would take it away from me. They forbade me to buy make-up and wear it at twelve-years-old, but that did not stop me; of course, I would go and buy it again. When I was twelve I looked sixteen, and that was what I wanted. I could not wait until I would be on my own and do what I wanted to do and eat what I wanted to eat.

Back to my story: The make-up business did not pan out too well, as I was using more than I was selling.

I was doing every kind of modeling that was available, including runway, print and showroom modeling. Show room work consisted of modeling lines of clothing for a manufacturer's representative. In Winnipeg, you could not make a living doing just one kind of modeling. You had to do it all. I was thinking about moving to Toronto where my father lived so I would have a much better chance at making more money as a model and becoming well known. Since I was on my own, my dad had divorced my mom and we now had an amicable relationship. Toronto was a much more cosmopolitan city with a greater population than Winnipeg and offered many more opportunities to work as a model.

I was modeling for Walter, a manufacturer's representative in Winnipeg. Walter became very interested in getting to know me better. I told him about my plans to move to Toronto, as I could not make enough money to live on in Winnipeg. He asked me not to move. He told me that if I stayed in Winnipeg, he would help me get a better apartment. I was living in a one bedroom with two kids. I gave my children the bedroom and I slept in the living room. It was crowded, and I really needed my own bedroom. Walter said he needed a friend, someone to talk to; but, of course, he had ulterior motives.

It was not long before we became sexually involved and he had me move into his friend's apartment complex. Walter was married. He told me how unhappy he was and that he wanted to leave his wife. His sister was dying of cancer and he could not ask for a divorce until she passed.

Walter wanted me to have a baby with him, but I refused to do that until he was divorced. He purposely tricked me when we were having sex and he got me pregnant. I was so naive. I had been on the pill for five years. I was having breakthrough bleeding and my doctor told me that I needed to go off the pill. I was off the pill and Walter knew this. We were using the withdrawal method for birth control. One dramatic moment, he did not withdraw and said, "I am going to make you pregnant," and he did.

I told Walter that if I was pregnant, I was going to have an abortion. My gynecologist told me to wait at least three months before testing since at that time, it was necessary to inject a rabbit with a woman's urine to do a pregnancy test. She said I had been on the pill for so long that I would probably miss at least three periods. By month four, still no period. I went and had the test. Dr. McFarlane said, "You are almost five months pregnant."

I said, "I'm getting an abortion."

She said, "No you're not, you could die."

I wept for weeks. I really did not want this baby. I think she sensed it when it was time for her to be born. Walter, on the other hand, was delighted. He was vacationing in Mexico with his wife; part of their winter ritual. I had his secretary give him the news. I came to grips with the idea that I was going to have another child.

Walter was twenty-five years older than I was. I was twenty-three-years-old and he was forty-eight. He was so proud of himself that he had made me pregnant. He asked me if I could help him look younger, as everyone thought I was his daughter. Well, he definitely came to the right place! I taught him about caring for his face. I would put eye cream on him and show him how to do facial exercises.

Our time together was limited and strained because he was married. We would sneak around with his secretary acting as decoy. I was pregnant and alone with my two children. I could not even tell my mother who the father of the baby was because of Walter's situation. We were waiting for Walter's sister to pass. It did not happen until two weeks before the baby was born. I was alone, hiding in my apartment for eight-and-a-half-months.

We finally moved in together and could stop hiding. At last, Walter had told his wife about the baby and me. Soon thereafter, our precious little girl Jessica was born. It was a horribly long, tedious delivery over a period of two days. It seemed like she did not want to be born. Finally she was coming! While I was in labor, the doctors poked their heads in and the nurse told them to go for lunch, as I had not dilated any more, but Jessica was coming fast and furiously. The nurse was hurrying so much that she forgot the IV bottle still attached to my arm. I was yelling, "hurry, hurry." In the delivery room, I barely had time to get on the delivery table before, with one huge push, she came out. At the exact same moment, the doctors came crashing through the doors just in time to get a blood bath from my self-delivery. No drugs, no nice episiotomy, just arrogant doctors who pronounced a spontaneous delivery. Spontaneous, my ass! I got ripped open, delivered without any doctor assistance, and I would later learn that my child suffered from oxygen deprivation at birth. I laid there in the fetal position crying and continued to do so back in my room for days. I felt so abused. Not only had they let me labor for forty-eight hours, but then when it was time for my baby to be born, they were not even there. What an ordeal! I told them how I felt, and they said that the next time I had a baby I could find another set of doctors. The next time; are you kidding me? You think I would ever go through that again? I always felt like something had gone terribly wrong. And, of course, later I would find out that it had.

My other two children, who were five- and seven-years-old, were happy about their new sister. Walter and I could not get married until his divorce was final. We lived half of the year in Palm Springs and the other half in Winnipeg. Walter wanted it that way, and he was definitely the boss. We lived an affluent lifestyle because he owned several businesses and was well off. It did not matter though, as he would remind me daily that nothing was mine. I lived in a beautiful home with a swimming pool and tennis court and a nanny. I could not have been more miserable. He was controlling and insanely jealous. I felt like I was in jail. What do beautiful things matter when your life is a living hell? Modeling and acting were out of the question, as Walter did not want me out of his sight. He abused me physically, mentally, emotionally and sexually. He was one big bully!

Mistreating me was one thing, but when he started to mistreat my children, I could not take it. I knew that this relationship was not going well.

Many odd incidents happened with Jessica. When she was a baby, sometimes her eyes would roll outward. I told her pediatrician and he sent us to an optometrist, who found nothing wrong with her eyes. There were other times when she would be sitting up and then slump to the side of her highchair. I would call her name and she would sit up. I did not think much more of it until one day, when she was around eighteen-months, I found her on the floor with her little butt in the air. I went to pick her up and she was having a grand mal seizure. All the little odd things went click, click, click, in my mind. She had been having these odd incidents since birth.

I was devastated. The diagnosis was she had suffered brain damage at birth due to lack of oxygen. Apparently, she had been stuck in the birth canal for too long. Perhaps she had felt unwanted. Oh yeah, remember the arrogant doctors who weren't there for her delivery? The damage included fine and gross motor disability, seizure disorder and mental retardation. We were overwhelmed.

We struggled for many years with our precious little girl. The doctors had trouble trying to control her seizures. They would try various drugs, and all of them seemed to have adverse affects on her. Walter and I could agree on nothing. Our constant fighting was affecting my children's lives. Their grades were going down and our house was in chaos. Walter would throw me out of the bedroom almost every night. Eventually, I started sleeping in the guest bedroom.

At this time, Jessica was five-years-old, Tommy was ten, and Sherry was twelve. Walter had tried to brainwash me during the time we were together. He would tell me how I could never make it on my own. He had me terrified of the freeways. However, despite my fears, one day I got in my car and drove to Los Angeles from Palm Springs. I filed for divorce. I was proud of myself. As soon as I served him, he simultaneously filed for divorce in Winnipeg. I was afraid of him. He was always screaming at me and trying to intimidate me. I did not care anymore. Anything would be better than the hell that I had been living in. He finally rented another home in Palm Springs and moved out.

Walter did whatever he could to get me out of his Palm Springs house. It was getting very hot in Palm Springs, so I took his offer to return to Winnipeg. He provided us with the townhouse we lived in before, plus a summer cottage at the lake. This was temporary of course, with the divorce pending.

Back in Winnipeg, I returned to modeling. My spirit was low, but my face looked great. At least I had taken care of my face, if not my soul. People would ask me if I had had my lips done. This made me laugh. I had always had big beautiful full lips. It was not always a good thing. As a child in school, they had called me blubber lips; well the joke was on them. Now they looked like the lips that every woman wanted. I learned how to do lip exercises to prevent lines around the mouth.

Beauty Tip #7 - Do lip exercises. Hold the corners of your mouth and try to blow out and flap your lips, making a BRRRR sound. Sort of the same way that horses do. It keeps the lips full and larger.

I looked good but felt empty inside. Why could I not find the keys to happiness? I looked at various alternative lifestyles, philosophers and religions. I was searching!

PART TWO

The Inner Transformation
(My Human Revolution)

CHAPTER 7

California Here I Come!
(Beauty Tip 8)

I could not take the cold winters anymore. I made plans to escape the frozen wastelands of Canada and head south to California, where I could pursue my dreams of becoming an actor. At one of my print gigs, I met a gorgeous creature. His name was William. We were in several shots together, and the heat between us was palpable. We talked afterward and ended up making out in the hallway next to the exit door. We exchanged numbers and soon started hanging out together. He neglected to tell me he was married. He was extremely bright and I shared my woes with him. I told him that Walter was having me tailed. William was very tall, and one night he chased after the private eye and kicked his windshield in. No one could intimidate William. I told him about my pending divorce. Walter already had a new girlfriend but he wanted to make me look bad in court. In Canada, at that time, they had Napoleonic laws. These laws favored men, and they had fault divorce. I could hardly afford a lawyer, let alone a private investigator. Walter tried to make me out to be a gold digger. I was on the witness stand for five days. Walter's lawyers questioned me from morning to night. I loved to dance. Some of my model friends and I would go to gay clubs because they played the best music. Of course, Walters's lawyers questioned me about what kind of clubs I frequented, insinuating I was gay. In the end, I got a fair settlement and I made secret plans to go to California. Walter was not happy. He hated me and wanted me to suffer. He took the divorce settlement to the court of appeals. Three of his friends sat on that bench. This court revised the original judgment. They left me with $50,000 and $1000 a month child support. They did not take into consideration that I had a handicapped child. I owed my lawyer $30,000. That left me with $20,000. Walter would pay me in Canadian funds so that I would get less every month, as the exchange rate would keep dropping to the point where I was only getting half of the agreed upon amount each month.

William and I made a plan for our secret escape. We did not want Walter to know, as he would definitely try to stop us.

At thirty-years-old, with three kids, a cat and a dog in a camper, William and I headed to California. I had stuffed that camper with everything; pots and pans, dishes, linens, you name it. We had a huge trunk on the roof that held all of our clothes. I had the worst migraine. I was so worried about getting over the border with so much stuff. If they had looked inside, we were toast! William was quite the talker, so he schmoozed with the border patrol officer about racing and we managed to slip on through.

We made it safely to California. I had made a previous trip to California to rent an apartment for us. When we got there, the apartment was not ready. We had to spend a few more days in the camper. I think the kids were excited and mad at the same time. I had taken them away from all their friends. They were used to moving though, because Walter and I had moved them back and forth from Winnipeg to Palm Springs for three years. We would live six months in Winnipeg and six months in Palm Springs.

After about a year, my boyfriend and I split. He was living a double life, one with me and one with his wife. He would go back and forth to Winnipeg. Hmm, what a surprise! You think that maybe there is a pattern here? Why did I keep getting involved with married men? It certainly was not my intention, and, of course, they never told me they were married until I was already involved with them.

Being the warrior that I had learned to be, I pulled my-self up by my bootstraps, lifted my chin and I continued my journey. I had developed a "never give up" spirit.

Beauty Tip # 8—Be Resilient! Roll with the punches. Take the lemons of life and make lemonade. A positive attitude is a beautiful thing and shows on your face.

CHAPTER 8

Costume Jewelry Business, Kids, Roomies, & Love Of My Life!

My first job in California was selling eyeglass frames to optometrists. I made a measly hundred dollars a week. I started going to acting classes, and before long I landed a couple of acting jobs. One of them got me my Screen Actors Guild (SAG) card, and the other my American Federated Television and Radio Artists (AFTRA) card. I was on my way; I was going to be a big star. Not so fast!

I struggled for years, barely making ends meet. One day, I bought some broaches from my friend Georgia's store. They were for my sisters for Christmas. Georgia told me I could go downtown and buy them from her friends wholesale. The dollar signs started going off in my head. I thought, if I can buy these for $5, I know I can sell them for at least $15. They were gorgeous. The wholesaler had fulfilled a large order for a chain of stores and was selling some of her leftover stock to me.

I set up a small briefcase with the sweater pins and the broaches. I would open it wherever I would go. Banks, restaurants, stores, and the women would go crazy. It was so easy. I was having fun and making money.

After a month or so, the owner asked me if I wanted to buy the remainder of her jewelry business. She included in the deal all of her stones, settings, parts, tools, various glues and stuff I would need to make the pieces. I was like a kid in a candy store. I could not wait to get started.

At this time, I was thirty-eight-years-old, and moved into a duplex in the slums of Beverly Hills. The slums here were the apartment buildings and houses on the border of Beverly Hills. My oldest daughter Sherry had met a rock star and wanted to move out on her own. She, too, wanted to be a rock star. It was a month before her seventeenth birthday. I was heartbroken, and cried for a year. On every holiday and event, I would miss her dearly. We had had a tumultuous relationship for years, so when she asked for my approval, I agreed. How could I refuse her when I had moved out at sixteen-years-old? She was very smart and strong willed. I wonder where she had gotten that? She had found a room to rent with one of my actor friends, so I knew she would be okay. My son Tommy remained with me as did my other daughter, Jessica. Tommy tried to fill his older sister's shoes. He had, unfortunately, gotten into smoking marijuana.

In order to pay the rent, I rented rooms to many different people. While I was out one night, one girl tried to seduce my boyfriend. To add insult to injury, she couldn't pay her rent. I asked her to leave. And she did, taking with her a lot of my grandmother's fine linens. One guy roommate, who was a friend of my son, was a real slob. I smelled something awful coming from his room. When I asked him what the smell was, he laughed and said he had spilled a quart of milk on the carpet. It had gone sour. GOODBYE! Having roommates was a horrible experience. I looked forward to the day that I could pay the rent myself.

To keep my singing chops up, I would go to different clubs at night and sing. The host would bring me up and I might get to sing one or two songs. One night, I was out with my girlfriends at a place called Romeo and Juliet's. I was waiting for my turn to sing. I noticed a very handsome man across the room. He was having dinner with his date, but we could not keep our eyes off each other. When his date went to the washroom, we really started staring at each other. They eventually left and I thought to myself, oh well, but moments later, the man returned. He walked up to me and asked me if he could take me out sometime, and handed me his card. I asked him if he was not already involved with the woman he was with, and he told me that she was just a friend. I asked him what he had told her when he left her in the car, and he said that he told her he wanted to meet me. I was shocked. He was very handsome like Omar Sharif, with a beautiful mustache and dark hair. He was shorter than I would have liked. I like taller men. Anyway, he was very good looking and I soon called him. His name was Anthony.

Anthony and I would have a ten-year relationship and I would have to say that he was the love of my life. The problem was that he did not want to get married. He said, "Not now, not ever, to anyone." That was clear, and he told me that on our second date. However, I thought, you know, he will fall in love with me and then he will want to marry me and then we will live happily ever after. Well, that did not happen, but we had a wonderful time together. We enjoyed each other's company. We respected and loved each other very much.

CHAPTER 9

Becoming a Buddhist
(Beauty Tips 9, 10, and 11)

Meanwhile, across town at another club called Dimples, my girlfriend CJ and I had a biweekly gig. Dimples was one of the first karaoke bar and restaurant places. CJ and I would host a karaoke show, and we had many followers. We were both funny and good-looking. We packed the joint. I was the better looking of the two, but she was a better singer. We used to bring other singers up to sing in between our numbers. One night, I was talking with one of the girls who was a fabulous singer. Her name was Diane. I was complaining to Diane that my friend CJ was singing more songs than me. I guess I was jealous. Diane told me very bluntly that I needed to chant!

I said, "Chant what?"

She handed me a piece of paper with words on it. She told me, "When you get home, just say these words repeatedly and it will really help you to become happy."

I did not realize at the time that this would be a defining moment in my life. This was the beginning of my inner transformation to find eternal happiness and joy.

46

Somehow, Diane had sensed my low life condition and my unhappiness. When I got home, I pulled out the piece of paper and started chanting the words that she had given to me. "Nam myo ho renge kyo," repeatedly I said the words and immediately burst into uncontrollable tears.

I did not understand why this made me cry. As I thought about it, I realized that I must have had so much suffering in my life, and for some reason these words had opened up the floodgates of my suffering. I was in disbelief. I called Diane and asked her what was happening to me. She invited me to attend a Buddhist meeting up in the Hollywood Hills. She lived in a beautiful house right under the "H" of the Hollywood sign. Diane told me that the home was a benefit due to her Buddhist practice and chanting the words that she had given to me. I was not quite sure that I believed her, but later, she revealed that she was taking care of the house in exchange for free rent. Wow, it was true. At first at the meeting, I thought the people were very weird. Then, after the chanting stopped, everyone started jumping up and down and celebrating. I was not sure what they were celebrating, but everyone there seemed to be so happy. Different people shared their benefits from practicing Buddhism, and they explained the practice to me. I was at such a low place in my life that at that point I would have tried anything. I had tried many different philosophies and religions over the years: Christianity, Judaism, Transcendental Meditation, Life spring, positive thinking and I even touched on Scientology. However, nothing brought me the joy that I was looking for.

Would this be the answer for me? Only time would tell.

Through the years, I had been taking care of my face and my body. I always exercised my body and my mind, but obviously, I had been neglecting my spirit. Although I had tried to find the key to eternal happiness, it had eluded me and no practices I had tried had brought me the peace that I was looking for. Could this finally be the key to what I'd been looking for?

Beauty Tip # 9- Exercise your spirit every day. Whatever your spiritual practice is does not matter; just make sure that you practice daily to maintain your happiness.

Beauty Tip # 10—Exercise your body and your mind every day. I play tennis and do yoga and Zumba, to name a few. To exercise my mind, I play word games where you have to come up with words on the timer. I also write, which is better exercise for the brain than reading. Exercising the body, the mind, and the spirit every day definitely shows on your face. These three elements are a necessary part of any beauty regiment.

Due to my newfound spiritual practice, I was in high spirits. I could not wait to get back to my newly purchased business. I was anxious to play with all the stuff I had purchased. I started putting the jewelry together and making different pieces. I came up with a few ideas of my own, and I was surprised how wonderful they were. My mother had always told me that I was not artistic because I could not draw as well as my older sister. It is a shame that parents say things like this, because it limits their children from believing in themselves. I soon discovered that not only was I artistic, I was very artistic. I was coming up with different designs and making things out of my head. I was so proud of myself and I felt so fulfilled. I read a book many years ago about the seven basic human needs, and one of them is to be creative. Being creative means many things. Creativity can take the form of acting, singing, writing and even business planning. Just because you cannot draw does not mean you are not creative. I remember being secretly annoyed at my mother for denying my creative abilities. Ultimately, through my Buddhist practice, I learned that we are all responsible for what happens in our lives. Blaming others does nothing to change our lives or take us in the direction we want to go. Taking responsibility for your own life is life changing.

Beauty Tip # 11—Take responsibility for your own life and what has happened to you. This is one of the most powerful things I have learned and was a turning point in my life.

CHAPTER 10

My Store On Melrose Ave.
(Beauty Tips 12 and 13)

My new boyfriend Anthony suggested that it would be nice for me to have my own little store where I could sell my jewelry. He was hell-bent on me having my own business. He was in real estate, and I was helping him to find listings for his commercial real estate business. I found one big buyer and we made a deal that took months. He found me a cute little space on Melrose Avenue. Melrose was a hot location at this time and the "in" spot to be. My store was long, narrow and small. I mirrored one side of the store so it would look bigger. I designed the store myself and made displays. I covered them with the same fabric that I covered the one wall in. I put padding underneath the fabric so that you could hook earrings into it. I took vertical pieces of mirror and placed them on the padded wall about three feet apart. These mirrors gave the customer a place to check out the earrings they were trying on. I was very proud of myself. Anthony and I found two nice jewelry cases, one smaller and one larger with sliding glass doors. The store could not take much more furniture. I set up my counter

51

desk so that I could look out and see the customers coming in. Below the counter was a lovely space where I would design and make my jewelry. I would sit there all day and work for hours on my orders and my new designs.

I had gotten some orders from some major department stores like Nordstrom's for their junior department. I was selling during weekends at Bullocks, doing trunk shows in their store. Business was slow in my little store, so I needed to go out on the weekends and sell elsewhere. It was great. I could just put a sign on the door as to when I would be back. The jewelry manager at Bullocks loved me so much that she gave me an open invitation to come and sell there whenever I wanted to. I had my own table, which I would put in the back when I was not there. One Christmas, I sold $40,000 worth of my merchandise in Bullocks department store. I stood on my feet eight hours a day, and then I would make stuff at night. I worked very hard. Unfortunately, that year Bullocks declared bankruptcy and did not pay me the $10,000 they owed me. I eventually got a settlement of $1,000. This almost put me out of business. I had worked so hard during the Christmas season, and now I had nothing to show for it. Fortunately, my spirits were high because of my Buddhist practice and my newfound spirituality.

I was able to secure five Saks 5th Avenue stores to carry my jewelry. This was a major coup for me. I had hired a cute woman as a salesperson. She worked at Saks 5th Avenue in Beverly Hills. She had many connections and she helped me obtain an order from Fred Hammond's in Beverly Hills. Fred Hammond's was the store that was the old Giorgio's. When the husband and wife split up, she moved down the street to her own store and he kept the location on Rodeo Drive and Wilshire Boulevard, and changed the name to Fred Hammond's. I designed special jewelry just for them. Mr. Hammond wanted some large round gold hoop earrings with his fragrance numbers inside, like Chanel, only with 247. Working with my manufacturer, we came up with a beautiful design and he ordered a bunch for his store. Later he had me design some beautiful gold lip pins. These were given out to all the guests at a special dinner party they were having. I bejeweled the lip pins with red crystal stones and they sold them in the store.

At one time, all the mannequins in their window displays were wearing my jewelry designs. It was my finest work ever. I designed gorgeous earrings, bracelets and brooches with multicolored stones in all shapes and sizes. I was so excited. I took pictures of the windows. I could not believe that the most famous boutique store in Beverly Hills had all their windows displaying my jewelry. This was the most prestigious, upscale expensive store where the rich and famous shopped. I had to pinch myself. I could not believe that my jewelry was actually in there. You might think that this was a very lucrative venture, but profits were somewhat spasmodic. My jewelry in Saks Fifth Avenue stores were on consignment only, so I was only paid when they sold merchandise. This newfound business was a real benefit from my Buddhist practice. I was working so hard on the jewelry business that I had put my acting career on the back burner. During this time of my life, I did that a lot. However, I was not going to lose sleep over. This brings me to my next beauty tips.

Beauty Tip # 12—Try to get at least seven hours of sleep a night. Sleeping is the time that your body rejuvenates, and your face as well.

Beauty Tip # 13—NEVER SLEEP ON YOUR FACE. Sleeping on your face causes wrinkles; nothing is more aging than sleeping on your face. I used to sleep on the side of my face, and one morning I woke up and I couldn't believe the lines that were pushed up around my eyes. I immediately forced myself to always sleep on my back, and if I find myself turning over, I wake myself up and I do not let myself sleep on my face. This is one of the reasons why I have looked ten to fifteen years younger than my age throughout my life.

My relationship with Anthony lasted for ten years. That is the same amount of time that I had my little store on Melrose. I asked Anthony's ex-wife why he would not marry me, and she told me it was because he was married to her. The whole time I had been living with him, he was still married to his ex-wife. He always told me that they were divorced. Once again, a married man had deceived me. I knew I could not stay with him anymore. One of our issues was that he was Persian. He always wanted me to cook Persian and be more like a Persian woman, and we had arguments about this. Although I was a good cook, I was not interested in learning how to cook Persian cuisine. In addition, I worked so hard that I felt as if he should take me out to dinner and not expect me to come home from work and prepare dinner for him. After all, he and his wife owned a restaurant. He was always saying, "The man should do this and the woman should do that."

Our cultural differences had begun to cause problems between us. Also, I realized that he was never going to marry me. I knew it was over.

CHAPTER 11

End Of Melrose and Anthony. Beginning of Mall and New Man.

I closed my store on Melrose because things were getting very scary. It was around the time of the LA riots over Rodney King. People were coming up and down the street and smashing windows. Then, one month, we had torrential rains and flooding that came in my front door. Melrose was not the wonderful cliché area it had been when I opened my store. Now, there were lots of homeless people and scary people coming into my store trying to sell me things. I did not feel safe there anymore and I wanted to get out.

Within the same two weeks I ended my ten-year relationship with Anthony and I closed my store that I had for ten years. I was scared. I started having panic attacks. Making these two big, catastrophic changes in my life at the same time probably was not a good idea. I started chanting more to regain my confidence and peace.

I was chanting for the wisdom to know where my next move should be. I decided that it might be fun to have a cart in one of the malls. I had my eye on Thousand Oaks, as there was a good community there and it was a nice place to work. It was getting closer to the holiday season and I thought it might be a great venue for me. I contacted the appropriate people at the Oaks mall and went to see their representative. I showed her my line of jewelry and talked about what I had hoped to do. She loved my stuff and said that it did not conflict with anything they already had in their carts. We came up with a contract for the rent and percentages they would be taking. I was so excited. The mall had its own designer who would design my cart. I would pay him the appropriate fee. We set a date and a time. The day before I opened, I worked for twelve hours. I had not heard from Anthony for two weeks, although he knew I was opening my cart. He offered little to no assistance to me. That is it, I thought to myself. I could have used his help to carry all the merchandise and displays into the mall. Then he could have helped me get ready for my opening the next day. I had to wait for the designer to finish getting the cart together, and then I was able to start preparing my displays. It was a big deal. I had a time restraint, and that is why I worked until midnight. I would have to be back there the next day at 7 a.m. Once you opened your cart, you could not leave. You had to be with it all day long. You might be able to go grab something for five minutes while someone else watched your cart, but you had to be there a certain number of hours each week. When the mall was open, your cart had to be, as well, otherwise they could fine you. That was the deal in the contract.

Through The Years Ages 1-9

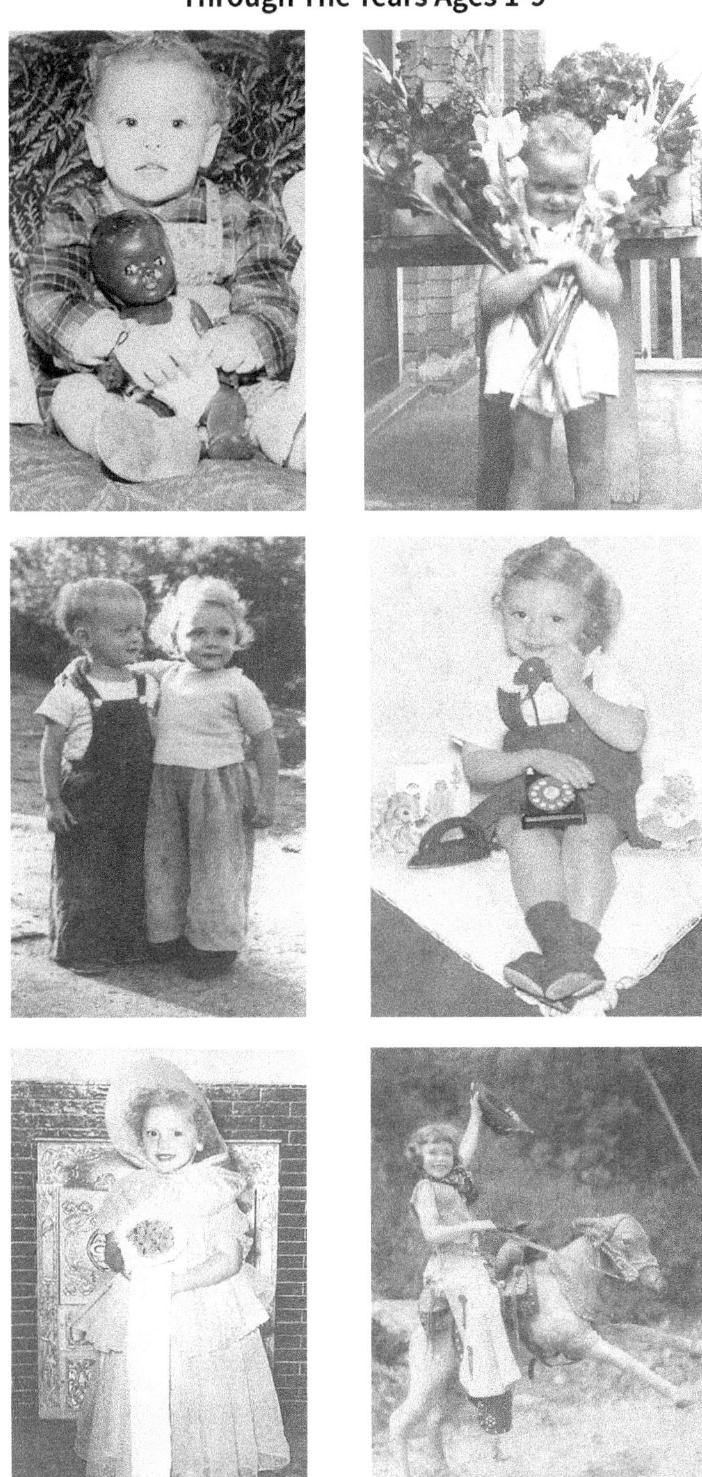

Through The Years Modeling 15 -32 Years Old

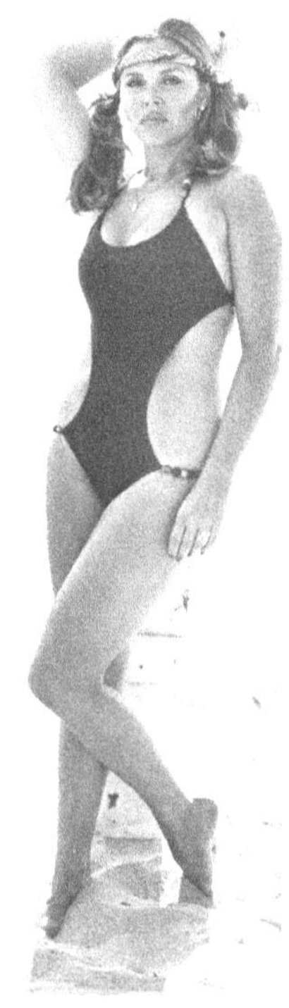

Air Force Pin Up Girl

FUNWEAR
the Bay
DOWNSTAIRS
BUDGET STORE
PERSONAL SHOPPING ONLY

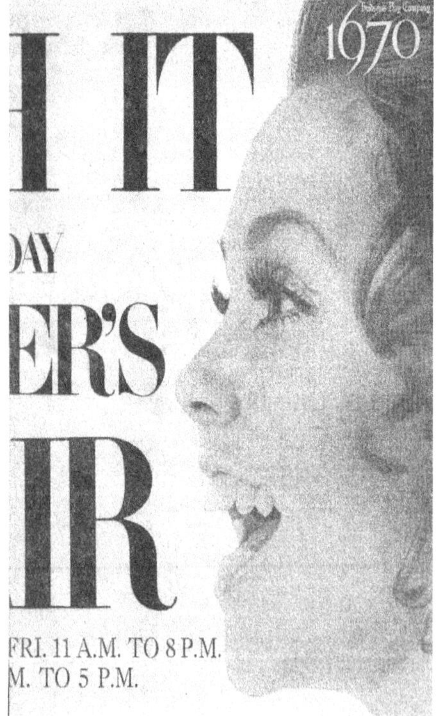
H IT
1670
DAY
ER'S
IR
FRI. 11 A.M. TO 8 P.M.
M. TO 5 P.M.

Le Mere
Fabulous Costume Jewelry
Designed
by
Vicki Le Mere
Wholesale Studio
7216 1/2 Melrose
(2 Blks. W. of La Brea)
(213) 937-9331

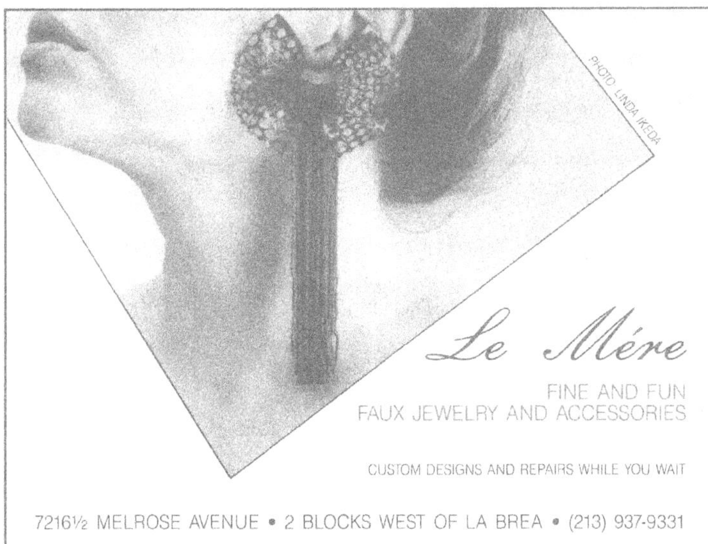
PHOTO LINDA IKEDA
Le Mére
FINE AND FUN
FAUX JEWELRY AND ACCESSORIES
CUSTOM DESIGNS AND REPAIRS WHILE YOU WAIT
7216½ MELROSE AVENUE • 2 BLOCKS WEST OF LA BREA • (213) 937-9331

Singing and Comedy Entertainment

My Family 3 Generations

My Family 3 Generations

Birthdays 4 Decades : 40 - 50 - 60 -70

With Love, Light & Remembrance

CHAPTER 12

Quick Proposal and Quick Marriage Equals Suspicions

The hours were beginning to kill me. I decided to hire some young women to help me out so that I could take a break occasionally. They unfortunately did not work out. Not only did they steal my merchandise, but they also did not sell anything, so I was losing money. The Christmas season was not as good as I had hoped for, and I found that I had to go out and sell at various other Christmas arts and craft shows. One day, after selling at Universal studios for ten hours, I came back to my cart and I was exhausted. A man approached my cart and said he needed some gifts for his daughters for Christmas. He said he had no one to help him wrap the gifts. I told him I was unfortunately out of boxes but if he would return the next day, I would wrap everything beautifully for him. His name was Greg; he was okay looking but nothing to write home about. At least he was tall, about six-foot-three-inch and certainly had the gift of the gab. He had a Russian man with him whom he told to go sit down in the corner. I looked awful after working that long day. I could not believe that he was flirting with me. I was slightly more interested when he flashed a black American Express card wrapped in wads of hundreds. Greg came back the next day and then asked me if I would go out with him. We set a date for that weekend. We had a wonderful date together, but Greg was a horrible kisser. It was like kissing a wall. I gave him his first kissing lesson. Obviously, whomever he had been with was not into kissing. He said that he could see good things for the future. I thought he was rushing a little bit, but it was also pleasant because I had spent ten years with Anthony with no plans for the future.

One day, while we were standing kissing by my cart, Anthony showed up. He was standing on the second level of the mall watching us make out. He was heartbroken. It was obviously over for us, but he had not talked to me in three weeks. God only knows what he was doing. He had a young woman move into his house that he said was just a friend who needed help. I never trusted the fact that he had her living there and that they were just friends. He was a very sexual person.

I felt badly for him, but I was not going to let it interfere with my newfound romance. Poor Anthony was devastated and lost thirty-five pounds. He did not need to lose even a pound and he looked awful. He wanted to be friends with us, but Greg would have no part of it.

For our third date, Greg said he had special plans. I was to leave work exactly half an hour before sunset and he would pick me up from the mall. I arranged to have someone work for me. Greg drove to the beach in Camarillo and he pulled into the parking lot overlooking the water. As the sun was setting, he turned to me and asked me to marry him. I was shocked! I thought it humorous. I told him that it was very premature and I would have to think about it, and he answered, I will take that as a "yes." Controlling and a little pushy, don't you think?

Well, here I was, at forty-eight; I had wasted ten years with Anthony. I had been waiting for someone to marry me for over twenty years, and now here was a man asking me to marry him on the third date. He gave me a ring and told me some cock and bull story about working for the FBI. He said that he had done some work for them and they let him go into the vault where all the confiscated merchandise was, from all different raids. He said that he had chosen this ring for me there. It turned out to be a fake, and so was he. I did not find this out right away, as I was in La La Land thinking that I had finally found my knight in shining armor. He told me he was doing secret service work and that I could not call his house because the phones were tapped. He did not answer his cell phone after 10 p.m.

Six weeks into our relationship, we planned a trip to Las Vegas. We stayed in the bridal suite, which should have given me a clue. He kept saying, "Let's get married, come on, let us just do it."

I was freaked out. I had waited twenty years to get married and I had never had a big wedding. I wanted a big wedding with all of my family from Canada there, and I was not going to ruin that dream. He kept pressuring me, and after two days I said, "Okay, but I still want my big wedding with all my family and I am not getting married now without a beautiful dress, flowers and the works."

Greg agreed to everything and whisked me off to Saks Fifth Avenue to buy a dress. We then went to a florist and got flowers. He seemed to know where all the spots were. He said we could get the license here and then go across the street to get wedding bands. Then, we could go to the little chapel over here and have a ceremony with a video and everything. It was as if he had done this before.

We got married but I did not want him not to tell anyone because I really wanted to have my big wedding. We planned it for six months later in the summer. Many weird things happened during the next six months. He would not let me come to his office. He kept making excuses. Then I told him I wanted to see where he lived. Greg said that he was helping a Ukrainian family because they had helped him do a big deal in the Ukraine. Apparently, they helped him purchase three tobacco plants for RJ Reynolds, the American tobacco company. Greg said he made $1.5 million for the deal and was re-paying this family by trying to help them get their green cards. He had rented a house in Thousand Oaks and was living with them.

Greg and I made a date for him to give me a tour of his house. It was a nice ranch-style home with two bedrooms and a Jacuzzi. Greg said that the Ukrainian couple slept in one bedroom and their daughter Lena slept in the other bedroom. Lena's room had a king size bed in it and the other bedroom had a queen size bed. I asked Greg where he slept, and he pointed to a couch in the hallway upstairs. I said, "This room has a king size bed and you are sleeping on the couch?" He told me he was hardly ever there because he was with me all the time. I thought it was odd; but it would only get odder.

Not long after the house tour, I got a call on our home phone from one of Greg's business associates. He said that he had met me in Carlsbad the previous week. I said, "I have never been to Carlsbad."

My heart sank. I confronted Greg as soon as he got home, but he shrugged it off, saying, "Oh, I was sitting next to Eli's wife and I guess he thought that was my wife."

Ha, ha right?

Soon after that, I had a small dinner party with Greg's accountant and his wife. We were talking about Las Vegas and various different things, and I said something about Greg not being married, and the accountant's wife Julie said, "Like hell he's not; I was at the wedding in Las Vegas."

I could feel my blood pressure rising. We needed to talk. As soon as our guests left, I confronted Greg. He told me he had to marry Lena, the Ukrainian couple's daughter, to help her get her green card. My marriage to Greg in Las Vegas had been a fraud, because he was already married to Lena, who was the same age as my daughter. He told me it was not a real marriage, that he was just trying to help them out. Yeah, right!

CHAPTER 13

Shady Husband. End in Sight.
(Beauty Tip 14)

Greg had many different business deals going on. A lot of them seemed shady. He would tell almost everybody he met about his Ukrainian businesses: Pepsi, water bottling, and clothing manufacturing. Apparently, he was using Pepsi's name without their approval, but I would not learn this until later. Almost everyone wanted to get in on his good deals, and of course, turns out they were all Ponzi schemes. He was a con artist of the highest level. He was constantly lying to me and making excuses for everything. He would use one lie to cover up another lie. It was very hard for me to decipher the lies from the truth.

Not knowing any of this at the time, I went ahead with our big wedding in August of 1994. My family came from Canada. It was an outrageously beautiful event. It was at the Ritz Carlton in Laguna Niguel, on a cliff overlooking the ocean. The setting was magnificent. My dress was magnificent. My husband, however, was an enigma. He had charged things on all my credit cards. He put this expensive wedding on my credit card, saying that he would

74

pay me back the following week when he got money for one of his deals.

The bullshit and lies continued for close to five years. One day, we were having a meeting at the house with one of my friends who was now involved with Greg. Greg's phone rang. I answered it, and there was a woman on the other line who asked to speak to her husband. I handed Greg the phone, and said aloud, "It's your wife calling."

I wanted my friend to hear that so he would know whom he was dealing with. This other wife was the Ukrainian daughter, Lena. He had married her in Las Vegas three months before he married me. I later found out that he had been seeing her and having sex with her the whole time we were together. One night we were out at a beautiful club for dinner and dancing. We were with my good friends, whom Greg was schmoozing. We were all doing the conga line. Greg was behind me, and all of a sudden I realized that he was not there anymore. He had disappeared. I sent my girlfriend's husband to the men's room to see if he was okay. He was not in the men's room. We could not find him and I was worried. After about forty minutes, he returned to our table and I asked him where had been? He said that Lena had come to the club. She had worked as a prostitute in Ukraine and I think she was on the prowl that night. I guess he made a mistake and told her where he was going to be. He probably told her that it was a business meeting and nothing about me being there. Oh, he was good! He had us both svengalied. He was trying to get my friends to help him do a business deal with Disney. He said he could have products made in the Ukraine that would be cheaper than China, then they could sell them to Disney. At this point, I did not realize how truly bad things were. However, he was my husband and I was trying to be supportive.

I soon came to realize that our marriage was doomed from the get go and I was going to have to figure out what to do. I wanted to cut my losses because he had maxed out my credit cards. In addition, the promise of paying them off just did not happen. One day I went to use one of my credit cards that should have had a $3000 available balance on it, but it was declined. I called the credit card company and they told me that I had been purchasing youth serums from Palm Springs every month to the tune of $500 a month, and that my card was maxed out. I was furious. I now had no credit cards left. Shortly after this, he had major surgery. He had 15 liters of ugly fat taken out of his body. He had an eyelift and he had his man boobs removed. The bill for this was $12,000, for which he just used money from one of his Ponzi schemes. He would get money from one investor and then he would pay the last person so he would keep the money rolling in and rolling out. The only one who was not paid was me. I was in so deep I did not know how I could get out. During our marriage, he married three other women. I did not even care. I was so over him. Not only was he a con artist and a liar, he was also a polygamist. Why had no one turned him in yet?

If it were not for my chanting, I think I would have ended up in the loony bin. Throughout all my trials and tribulations with Greg, I kept my spirit up by chanting. He could take away my money but he could not take away my happiness. People always told me what a beautiful smile I had. We would have chanting meetings at my house, and one of my seniors told me that when I smile, I light up the room. Here is my next beauty tip:

Beauty Tip # 14 - SMILE! It is good for your face and good for your soul. I read somewhere in one of my many studies **that it takes 47 muscles to smile and only seven to frown. So not only is it infectious when you smile, it also is good exercise for your face. Keep smiling and happiness will follow. When you smile, people smile back.**

I started thinking about how we were going to end this horrible mess. Greg had maxed out my credit cards. His word meant nothing; I could not count on him for anything that he had promised me. To save money, he wanted us to do our own divorce. We went to one of those legal help places. I was trying to drag things out as long as possible, because it was getting close to our five-year anniversary. In order to get any kind of spousal support, one needed to be married for five years. I was not going to let him off the hook that easily. He was seeing two other women. When he finally moved out, he moved in with both of them. Neither one of them knew that he was staying with the other one. He was so arrogant and full of himself that he was actually living with both of them, in the same complex, five blocks away from each other. He would tell one that he was going out of town and go stay with the other one and so on and so on. They were both Ukrainian women; Reina and Yasmina. I think they were desperate and needed someone to take care of them. Good luck to them.

Greg kept pressuring me about the divorce and I kept stalling, as I wanted the five years to pass. Finally, the time came and we split. I had introduced Greg to horse racing. It was unfortunate because he became a sick gambler. One week we were sitting in our box, and the next week he had another woman sitting in our box in my chair. He had no respect for me or probably any other woman. Although we were done, this really hurt my feelings. The body was still warm, if you know what I mean. Give it some time or at least be respectful. Do not show up in public with another woman and have her sit where your wife sat the week before, where she had sat for five years. He was a piece of work.

With all the action he had going on, he still wanted to get together with me. What a joke. I humored him with lunches and dinners just so that I could keep things on cordial basis.

He used to go to bed early, like 9:00 p.m., and I was a night owl. After I knew he was out cold, I would go through his briefcase and his journal so that I knew exactly what was going on in our lives. He was making a plan to disappear. He had the books and all the materials needed. One book was *How to Become an Anonymous Person*. It seemed like he was going to screw everybody. I was not sure if I was included in that list. I could not trust him as far as I could throw him, which was not very far because he weighed over 220 pounds.

Of course, I was right. He left me with a check for $5,000, which immediately bounced, and he was off to another country with another woman; this one was Ilena. The rent for the house that we were living in was $3,000 a month, so I immediately told our property owner that I would have to leave. Apparently, Greg had gotten them involved in one of his schemes and they did not yet know what was about to happen. I did not have that kind of money. He really did a number on me and many other people, as well.

PART THREE

The Outcome—Looking and Feeling Great As You Age!

CHAPTER 14

Rising From My Ashes, Letting Go
(Beauty Tip 15)

Like the phoenix, they say that Scorpios rise from their own ashes. Well, I rose and said, "Goodbye ashes!"

I rented a little house and got on with my life. One of the things I learned from my Buddhist practice was to never give up. I think that I naturally had that in my DNA, but I needed help bringing it out. It helps so much in life if you can be positive. It shows on your face and makes you look more youthful and beautiful. So let us have another beauty tip:.

Beauty Tip # 15 - As Winston Churchill said, "Never give up. Never ever ever!" Try to think *positively* about everything, because being negative only brings you negative results.

It was early in 1999 that I made my move. I rented a nice three-bedroom house. I was 52, but I felt so much younger than my age and looked much younger, as well. People thought I was in my early forties or late thirties. Well, here I was with another new beginning! Living in a big house, I had accumulated a lot of clothing. When I went to move, I had fifteen wardrobes full of clothing. After five, I told the mover there was no more room and he said he had 10 more wardrobes. God I loved clothes. Greg had always encouraged me to shop as much as I wanted ... I guess he was trying to deter my attention from whatever he was doing. It all seems so long ago now and I was so happy to be free of him and his cons.

By this time, my children were pretty much on their own. I had been encouraged to help Jessica become more independent and to let her go. I went through a very hard transition trying to do this. It took me three years of therapy and a lot of encouragement from her doctors and social workers. I cried a lot. I had feelings of guilt and failure as a mother. However, I soon came to grips with the fact that she needed to grow and so did I. My other two children needed me too, and I had given a lot of my time and energy to Jessica. Jessica would come home every weekend and was adjusting to the new program.

I like to mention at this time that the doctors told me that Jessica would not live much past thirty-years-old. Today, I am proud to say she is forty-nine-years-old and a very happy healthy young lady. Although her mental age is around five-years-old, she really enjoys her life. She is mostly in a wheelchair and walks with a walker, with some difficulty. She has very bad balance. I encourage her to walk although, like most of us, she's lazy and would rather not. She likes to do puzzles, color and watch movies and videos.

Tommy was on his own and had custody of his two daughters. They spent a lot of time with grandma and had their own rooms and their own beds in my house. I was more of a mother to them than a grandmother. However, that is a whole other story. Tommy loved to work on cars. He had found a small spot to rent. When I saw the joy on his face when he showed it to me, I knew he was doing what he was supposed to do.

Sherry had her own band and a day job to support her love of music. She came to realize that she might not be able to make a living as a singer, and asked me if I would help her go back to school so that she could become a doctor of Chinese medicine. She had to finish her undergraduate degree before she could start the Yo San University of Traditional Chinese Medicine program. She is extremely intelligent and I am very proud of her. She got her decree and started working as a Doctor of Chinese Medicine. It was not an easy task for her, and took many years of studying and working part time. At night, I would go to all of her gigs and dance like a crazy fool. Oh dear, there I go regressing again.

CHAPTER 15

Reaching Out— Helping Others
(Beauty Tip 16 17 and 18)

From the time I started chanting until now, I had always been a Buddhist leader in my community. It is not a position of authority; more a position of responsibility for helping other people. This has been part of my human revolution; the way I changed from the inside out. Helping others has always been my benefit. You cannot light a light for another human being without shining a little light on your own life. The high you get from helping another human being who is suffering is one of the greatest feelings I have ever experienced. People ask me,"What is it about you? I see a light in your eyes."

I smile, as I know the light is my Buddha nature shining from inside of me. It comes partially from helping other people and from helping me, as well. I think it is time for another beauty tip:

Beauty tip number #16—Help other people who are suffering. It will help lessen your own suffering and make you more beautiful.

Greg had fled the country with his new love. During the time that we were married, Greg had not wanted me to work. He always told me that we were affluent. What a joke! He ended up owing me $350,000. I could say that he ruined my life, but I was not going to play the victim role anymore. Besides, I never felt that way. My life was my responsibility and I was not going to let anyone con me or pull me down again. I was determined. I would never ignore red flags again.

I had a girlfriend come and stay with me for a little while. She rented one of the rooms. She was an actor like myself, but very self-absorbed. She did give me one great beauty tip, though. She told me to stop plucking my eyebrows so thin. She said it made me look older. Done! No one had to tell me a good tip more than once, especially one that would help me look younger. She did not last too long as a roommate though, because she could not pay the rent and, oh yeah, one day I came home and found her in bed with my 15 year old son. I finally had to throw her out; literally. However, I will always be grateful for her beauty tip.

Beauty Tip # 17—Do not pluck your eyebrows too thin, or remove them all together and draw a fake line. Nothing ages you more than that look. If you have no eyebrows, have them tattooed in tiny brush strokes or draw them in, that way.

This tip goes hand in hand with the one above so I thought it would be a good time to include it. This I discovered on my own when noticing that I did not like the way eye shadow looked on me anymore.

Beauty Tip# 18—Stop wearing eye shadow when you get older, it makes you look older, especially the glitter kind. If you are going to wear eye shadow over fifty, wear a neutral matte color.

CHAPTER 16

New Home, Selling Jewelry, Notary Public, One Woman Show

I started concentrating on my jewelry business again. I would do arts and craft shows and various other venues just to make ends meet. The woman I was renting my house from suggested that it might be great for me to get my own house. She had found a cute little house in a cul-de-sac that she thought maybe I could handle. I did not have much money, only about $15,000 in the stock market. I took that money out, and the next week the stock market crashed. I think I had good timing or was it good karma! I was able to purchase the house on a lick and a prayer. It was at a time when they were allowing people to buy homes with stated income. I barely made it. I had to accept a very high interest rate of 8.75 percent. The mortgage payments along with all the credit card payments that Greg had left me with were just about wiping me out. I struggled to pay the mortgage for quite some time.

Then I did something I said I would never do. I declared bankruptcy. I just could not take the late fees, the over the limit fees and I could see no other way out of this financial dilemma. I have seen so many people do this before and I thought it was disgusting, and now here I was doing the same thing.

Luckily, I was able to keep my house. Although I struggled to make ends meet, I always seemed to have enough money to get by. I was consistently able to make a living without assistance from anyone. I think I owed this in part to my consistent Buddhist practice and helping other people. I was never afraid. I somehow managed to be optimistic, even when things were tough. Let us face it; the birds do not worry about where their next meal is coming from. They trust that the universe will take care of them.

I started selling my jewelry in beauty salons. This worked out very well for me. At the salons, I had a captured audience of women walking around with color on their hair and nothing better to do than buy my jewelry. It was great. I spent five years each in three different salons and made a decent living.

I had a cousin in Northern California who was a notary. She was making over $1,000 a week. I thought to myself, this is a great idea. I went to notary school, got my license, and started doing notaries on the side. I worked for a company that took 60 percent of each job and only gave me 40 percent. Many times, all I made was $19 per job and I had to pay for my own gas. It was not enough. I eventually started to find my own customers. It was much more lucrative that way.

Life was good. I had my jewelry business, I had some notary work and I was doing odd acting jobs here and there. I loved entertaining and making people laugh. My dream entertainment job was to be able to sing, do comedy and dance. That dream came true when I put together a little cabaret act and performed at a local dinner nightclub place called the Gardenia Café in Hollywood. It was a sweet little dinner club and many famous people had performed there, including Ella Fitzgerald. I also had the pleasure of doing comedy at The Comedy Store on Sunset Boulevard. I probably performed there at least twenty times. In addition, I performed at other comedy venues like the Improv on Melrose Avenue and the Ha Ha Café in North Hollywood. I did not have to do the usual open mic nights. I was past that point. I was a good enough comedian that I would get booked shows.

CHAPTER 17

Match or Mismatch
(Beauty Tips 19, 20, & 21

My life was full. The only thing missing was a partner. I had been dating off and on for many years when I met a guy on match.com. We seemed to hit it off. He took me out to dinner on our first date, and we seemed to have some nice chemistry. On our second date we met at his home, which was nice. He was the vice president of a big insurance company and good looking. He had a nice body, as well. I thought I had met my dream man. Although he liked to drink, I never saw him acting belligerent. We did many fun things together, mostly going out to eat and dancing at one of his regular hang out bars. This was new to me, except for the dancing part. But what the heck, I was in love. We went to Las Vegas a lot. It was one of my favorite places in the world. George had business associates who would take him out all the time and he would give them business in return. We had been dating for about a year when he asked me to marry him. I said yes. Shortly thereafter, I moved in with him. That is when I saw the reality of the situation. This man had a serious drinking problem. I saw a side of him that I had never seen before; he was "a falling down drunk." He was a total alcoholic.

I had rented my house and sold all of my furniture and everything I owned down to the toaster, microwave and iron. The only things I had brought with me were my golden retriever and my personal effects. I had rented and not sold my house. Thank God, I did not sell it. We had set a wedding date for three months after my move. After about a month of living together, I knew that we were not going to get married. Even though I had the dress, the caterer and everything like that, I told him we needed to go for counseling and he agreed to it.

The therapist told him that he could not lie to me and get angry with me for no reason. She gave him homework to do to find out where his anger was coming from, but he never did it. He never told me he did not do it. The afternoon of the day he was supposed to go to therapy, he went straight to a bar. He never told me this, but the therapist did. Apparently, he did this a lot. I found out that he would leave work around 3 p.m. and then go to "titty bars." He really did not want to work on himself. He told me that he loved to drink. One night when he was drunk, which seemed like every night, George told me his dream life would be to own a bar and to get so drunk that at the end of the evening, one of his employees would have to walk him upstairs and help get him into bed. At this dream bar, he would have naked women walking around and sports playing on the television and people playing pool. I wish he had told me this vision before I had moved in with him.

Now I was rather stuck because I had rented my house for a year and I had this big golden retriever. No one would allow me to rent an apartment with this big dog. We knew we were not going to stay together, but we were still sleeping together. He went off to Florida for a vacation with his friends. I noticed he took his Viagra with him, so I knew he was cheating on me, as well. It was torture staying there knowing that I was leaving. I still loved him, even though he was an alcoholic. I was in love with him before I found out he was an alcoholic.

We planned to part as soon as I got back into my house. Once again, I had ignored the red flag of alcoholism. I had told myself that he was a happy drunk, unlike my father who would get nasty when he was drunk. I never saw this side of George until I moved in with him.

Through the years, I have noticed that people who drink a lot look weathered and older than their age. I never liked to drink much. Possibly because I was prone to migraines and that was a trigger for me. Therefore, it is time for my next Beauty tip:

Beauty Tip # 19—Do not drink too much. Getting drunk and having hangovers will age you dramatically.

George's previous girlfriend was a drinker and a heavy smoker. Even though she was ten years younger than I was, she looked ten years older than I did. She used to tell everyone that I had had multiple facelifts. I had never had any! Ha! Pursing your lips as you draw on a cigarette causes awful permanent lines around the mouth. There is no reversing the deep lines. Do you sense a beauty tip coming?

Beauty Tip # 20—DO NOT SMOKE! Next to the sun, it has the most aging effect on the face. If you do not want to stop for your health, which is a damn good reason, at least stop for your looks, your beauty. SAVE YOUR FACE.

I finally moved back into my house. What a joy it was to be there. You would think I would be upset after breaking up a five-year relationship with a man that I loved. Well, I was not; I was relieved. I felt fortunate, as if I had dodged a bullet. Although I loved George, I knew that if I stayed with him the future would not have been happy. I wanted my "happy ever after." I was not going to settle for less.

Beauty Tip # 21—Do not let anyone take away your happiness. Do not stay in an abusive or unsatisfactory relationship. Life is too short for that!

CHAPTER 18

Looking Good, Feeling Great, Working Out!
(Beauty Tips 22 & 23)

Through the years, I have managed to look good and feel good. I always did my chanting every day and helped other people to do so, as well. Even when I lived with George, I would have people over to the house to chant. It was always a lovely experience.

I was alone, but I did not feel alone. My spiritual being filled me up. I was at a good place. I did not *need* a man in my life but I *wanted* a man in my life. That was a good place to come from; wanting not needing. It seems like I had come full circle. I remember that many years ago when I found a man, I would be like a cling-on vessel. Eventually, he would peel me off and throw me away. It is so good to feel your own power and be in the driver's seat of your life. There was a time when the universe was slapping me around like a rag doll. Now I was in control of my own destiny.

Beauty Tip # 22— Love yourself. Until you do, no one else will. Develop self love. Affirmations, acts of kindness to yourself. For example, get a massage.

I want to mention here the importance of exercising. Although I mentioned it in tips 9 and 10, I think it bears repeating. I have always exercised. I feel it is an important part of a beauty routine and a spiritual routine. Exercise relieves stress, and who doesn't need to have less stress in their lives today? It might not be for you and that is perfectly fine.

When I was in junior and senior high school, I did every sport possible. I played volleyball, basketball, I ran track and did field events. I have many ribbons from those days. One year when I got into discus, I broke the city record for my division and went on to the provincial championships. I broke the record with the longest throw ever thrown, in my division, but, because I was so excited, I unfortunately stepped out of the wrong side of the circle. I knew that I had broken the record. My father was filming the whole event from behind me. I was jumping up and down and went out the wrong side of the circle. I was unfortunately disqualified!

This was probably the only regret I had in my life. Knowing how my life went, you probably find this hard to believe.

I truly treasure my struggles; they have made me so much stronger. They have made me who I am today.

Back to the sports. I loved sports and I loved competition. I played baseball for nine years. I was a pitcher and a shortstop. I could not wait to get outside at recess so that I could play baseball. In addition, after school I would stay and play "work your way up" baseball. I loved it. I was not so happy about schoolwork in general, but I loved the athletic component of school. I am not saying that you have to like sports or be involved in them to look good or live long. All of my grandparents lived into their nineties and none of them did any planned exercise.

I eventually started dating again, and although I had many mini-relationships through the years, I have not met the man with whom I want to spend the rest of my life. Online dating is horrible. It is such an unnatural way to meet someone. Everyone lies about his or her age, his or her height, his or her hair, but mostly about his or her size. I could tell you such stories about some of my disaster dates, but I have already written a book about that. It is a bathroom book called *Vicki's Dating Disaster Diary*. Only the weird and the absurd made the pages. Over the years, I have had so many first dates, but unfortunately, I have not yet had my last date. He is still out there. I know I will meet him someday. I believe in love.

Beauty Tip # 23— Keep your sense of humor about everything. Learn to laugh at yourself and see the humor in your disasters.

CHAPTER 19

Why I Wrote This Book

Today, I am happy, healthy, vital, beautiful and alive at seventy-five. I felt compelled to write this book because I have wanted to share my secrets for a very long time. I really felt like I had something; something I believe to be the keys to looking and feeling great in your senior years. This is what has worked for me. I am not saying that it will be the answer for you, but what do you have to lose by trying?

When I was nineteen-years-old, the only thing I wanted was to look great then and amazing when I got older. That was the beginning of my quest to look a lot younger as I aged; a conscious desire of mine. The inner work would come later. At nineteen-years-old, I had no idea that the biggest gift I would be able to give myself would be to change on the inside. This was the key to becoming truly beautiful and happy.

These are my revelations, the things that happened in my life's journey, to make me write this book:

- I was stopped by the police when I was in my thirties because they did not think I was old enough to have a driver's license. At that time in Canada, you had to be sixteen years of age to get your driver's license.

- I was having dinner with my youngest daughter at Islands Restaurant. I was in my fifties. I ordered a margarita and the girl asked me for my ID. I bent her over backwards and gave her a big kiss. Just kidding, I did blow kisses at her though. I thanked her and I showed her how old I was. It was such a hoot.

- I had a dear friend whom I just lost to Covid-19. We were friends for over twenty-five years. Twenty years ago in Las Vegas, we took a picture together at a show. He was an entertainer, as well. Twenty years later (two years ago) we took a similar picture so that we could compare them. I had hardly changed and he looked pretty darn good as well. The only difference was that he had about $100,000 worth of plastic surgery. The pictures are in my book. My dear friend Marcel, I love you with all my heart, I miss you terribly.

- About fifteen years ago, my friend Marcel told me that if I had plastic surgery, I would look younger than my children. Marcel used to say that I was a freak of nature because of how young I looked for my age.

- When I would go out with my oldest daughter people would ask if we were sisters. She did not like it very much but I loved it.

- When I would go out with my son, they always assumed I was his girlfriend. He was proud of it.

- About nine years ago, I found a new gynecologist whom I liked very much. The first time I was in her office she said, "Okay, before we talk about anything, I need to know all your secrets and how you can look so young for your age, which I see here right in front of me?" I laughed and told her that I really appreciated your comments. She said, "No, I am serious, I really want to know what you do, I want to know your complete routine." I was there recently to see her and she told me that I had to go on TikTok and make videos and share my secrets with the world. She actually was instrumental in me writing this book because she always felt like I had some secrets that I needed to share. The last comment she made to me was, "You defy reason!"

- Five years ago, I was having a mammogram and a similar situation happened. The technician said, "I see here that you are seventy-years-old and I don't believe that. So could you please tell me how it is that you could look so young when you say you never have had plastic surgery? What have you done to stay looking so young?" Once again, I laughed and I told her that I would tell her some of my secrets before I left.

- For the past twenty years or so, whenever I tell people how old I am their jaws literally drop and they are speechless.

- A week ago, I was having lunch with my youngest

daughter at a place where I have been going for over twenty-five years; a little sandwich shop in a strip mall where I have been working. I know the owners well, and the other day one of them asked me if I would mind telling her how old I was. When I told her I was seventy-five, she just stood there with her mouth hanging open and said, "No way, oh my God, you look so good, you need to tell me right now everything that you know and how you stay looking so young?"

- These occurrences happen to me every day. Every time I get an opportunity, if someone compliments me on something, I always say, "Not bad for a seventy-five-year-old, right?"

It is so rewarding to be complimented on a regular basis, and it is so important for me to share these secrets and tips with the world. Everyone needs to be able to look her very best at every age, and there are things we can do to help ourselves. Of course, my spiritual practice is the essence of my beauty and one of the reasons why I look so great for my age. There are many more things you can do to look great as you age. Whatever age you are, start now to save your face. Find your peace and happiness on the inside. Take care of yourself from the inside out. These are some of the keys to looking beautiful and feeling good into your seventies.

PART FOUR

Encounters

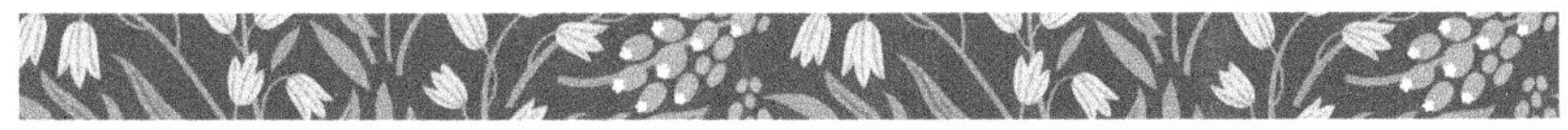

CHAPTER 20

The Le Mere Jewelry Story

I started my jewelry business in 1984. It was actually kind of a fluke ... Or was it? It was at the same time that I had just begun my Buddhist practice and I was feeling empowered.

As mentioned previously, I started with just a few items that I purchased downtown. It turned into me buying the rest of Carol's inventory and starting my own business. With my then boyfriend, Anthony, we found my cute little store on Melrose Avenue. My store on Melrose was a dream come true.

Melrose was the trendy "in" spot to be, and my jewelry store had a Betsey Johnson store right across the street from the first Johnny Rockets. Many other trendy restaurants and boutiques opened up, and my neighbor to one side had a hand-made designer shoe store. Many celebrities were drawn to the area because of the array of wonderful stops and restaurants. Everybody who was anybody wanted to go to Melrose Avenue.

In this little space, I created many of my most beautiful designs and I met some of Hollywood's biggest stars.

CHAPTER 21

Le Mere Jewelry and Celebrities

Nicolas Cage came in one day looking for a gift for a friend. He looked very handsome and was rather shy. We managed to find something wonderful for him. I gift wrapped it and we talked about a mutual friend of ours. He left quickly as if he wanted to get out of there before anyone would notice him. That was the nice thing about my store; it was small and intimate, and people felt safe coming in there. I usually did not have too many customers at the same time.

Penny Marshall of (Laverne and Shirley) fame was also very quiet and shy. It was as if she did not want me to recognize her. She spoke very few words and eventually picked out a simple bracelet for herself and left quickly.

Joyce De Witt, from *Three's Company* was adorable. She sat down on one of my high top chairs by my counter and we had the nicest long conversation. It was as if we were girlfriends. She told me all about the show and things that went on there that I cannot discuss, but it was very interesting, to say the least. She purchased some lovely earrings and she said she would come back soon.

My favorite celebrity customer ever was Joni Mitchell. She was one of the nicest people I ever met; but why not? She was a fellow Canadian, and you know that Canadians have a reputation for being really nice people. Joni was from Saskatchewan, which is the next province. I am from Manitoba. They are probably the two coldest provinces in Canada. We shared war stories about the cold and the winters. We were having a good old laugh. I asked her about her life and she told me about her love stories. It felt like we were kindred spirits. She was born in McLeod, Saskatchewan. It was a small town. She was a small town girl with a big town heart. I told her I had an idea for a song based on a recent experience that I had. I was at a wedding in Whistler, British Columbia, and I met a guy at a local bar. We kind of hit it off and we kept in touch over the months and we eventually made a plan to meet in Las Vegas. We went on a roller coaster there and I lost my favorite hat. I told her that the name of the song was "I lost my hat, I lost my head, and I lost my heart." Joni thought it was hysterical and a good idea for a song. I will never forget the time I spent with Joni Mitchell; one of the greatest female singer/songwriters of all time. Love you, Joni.

Eric McCormack from *Will and Grace* bought something from me at a street fair I was doing around Christmas one year. It was an outdoor street fair and I was so cold I cannot even remember what he bought.

Over the years, I designed and manufactured an array of gorgeous jewelry. Some of the major stores that I sold to were: Bullocks, Macy's, Robinson May, I magnum, Nordstrom's, Saks Fifth Avenue, and some prestigious boutiques like Giorgio's/Fred Hammond's, in Beverly Hills.

I worked one day a week at a lingerie store up in the Mulholland area. It was a very exclusive little area, and many stars came up there to have their clothes altered and go to the various restaurants. The woman that owned the store divided it into two parts. One-half of the store was for alterations and the other half for lingerie. You had to walk through the lingerie store to get to the alterations department. How clever that was, as customers would often stop to look at merchandise on their way to alterations. I really did not want the job, but she needed someone only one day a week. I told her I would work for her if she allowed me to display some of my jewelry there. I gave her half of everything I sold so it was good for her, as well. She agreed.

Many celebrities frequented that area. They would come in to have their clothes altered. The woman I worked for, Gayle, did excellent alterations. One of the most famous people who used to frequent the store and the alteration shop was Priscilla Presley. While paying for her alterations one day, she noticed my jewelry and admired a large cross necklace that I had. It was crusted with crystal stones that looked like diamonds, emeralds, rubies and sapphires. She was very soft-spoken and rather shy, but she got excited about this piece. She told me that she was going to take it to her jeweler and have him copy it with real diamonds, sapphires, rubies and emeralds. Whoa, I thought to myself; that is going to cost a fortune. I told her I thought it was a great idea. She bought the piece and frequently returned to the counter where I worked. I think she felt safe and comfortable around me, as I did not fuss over her as if she was a star, even though she was and I admired her. She was beautiful and kind and a lovely person.

Another star customer of mine was Teri Hatcher of *Desperate Housewives* fame. She would come into the store frequently, mostly for alterations but occasionally she would purchase something from me. One day she came in with her daughter who was about eight years old. The daughter wanted certain things and Terri told her to put it on her wish list for Christmas. I loved the fact that she did not just buy her daughter whatever she wanted, she made her respect the value of things. I remember her being a wonderful mother and a gorgeous woman.

Natalie Cole also frequented the lingerie store and the alteration shop. She loved my costume jewelry and purchased several things from me. She was stunningly beautiful and was a lovely kind person, as well.

One year I made all the jewelry for a beauty pageant that Lisa Gibbons was hosting. Another time I made all the jewelry for a play at the Ahmanson Theater. It was for a Victorian-style performance, so all the jewelry had to be antique looking and I had all the pieces needed to accomplish that feat.

Over the years, my jewelry business has morphed into more of an import/export business. Although I will design special pieces to order, the mainstay of my business now is buying and selling. My business came to a screeching halt during the pandemic, as did my acting and performing gigs.

I recently have started to sell some jewelry again. I am continuing after thirty-seven years in business. Yippee!

CHAPTER 22

A Date With Warren Beatty

When I was a girl of approximately thirteen years of age, I had a huge crush on a movie star that I saw in my mother's movie magazines. His name was Warren Beatty, and I thought he was a dreamboat. He had dreamy eyes. I cut out every picture of him from the magazines and put them on my wall beside my bed. I used to look into his face and those starry eyes and I would just swoon.

Fast forward twenty-five years or so, and I was living in the slums of Beverly Hills with my three children, trying to make it as an actress in Hollywood. I had booked some small parts in movies and television and I had received both of my union cards. I was a working actor, so to speak. One night, unexpectedly, I had a profound dream. In that dream, I was with Warren Beatty. It was so clear and I had this feeling as if I was going to meet him. I told a friend of mine about my dream. She was in real estate and she knew many very famous people. She looked at me and said, "I know him, do you want to meet him? I think he would really like you."

I said, "Of course I want to meet him. I've been waiting my whole life to meet him!"

It was all surreal. She arranged a luncheon at the Beverly Wilshire Hotel, in a little restaurant in the back of the main lobby. It was well known that Warren had a penthouse in that hotel and resided there some of the time. He was late, of course, and I was surprisingly not too nervous, as I felt like this was some sort of destiny. He walked in, took one look at me, and said, "Let's go."

I insisted that he sit down and talk to me. He did for a brief moment and then took me by the hand and led me off.

Our encounter is for my memory only. It is not something that I want to share with the world. He would call me from time to time. Although I had his phone number, I never called him. I knew who he was and what I was to him. I got what I wanted. I got my fantasy. I was happy, I was very happy. This encounter was the fulfillment of a childhood dream; a dream that came true. I was able to meet my childhood movie star crush, my dreamboat. He was gorgeous and I remained on cloud nine for a very long time.

CHAPTER 23

My Time with Natalie Wood

Sometime in 1973, I went to check out a nursery school for my daughter Jessica, who was three-years-old at the time. It was called the Leisure Loft. It was located just outside of Palm Springs where I lived with my then husband and my two other children. My other children were approximately eight- and ten-years old. We spent the winters there to get away from the cold in Canada.

Upon arriving at the nursery school, I sat in the back of the room and let my daughter interact with the other children to see if this place was a good fit for her. I looked over and saw a very cute girl lying on her stomach, perched up on her elbows. She had dark hair up in pigtails and was wearing sunglasses. I kept thinking, "God she looks familiar."

As I looked a little longer, I thought to myself, "Wait a minute, that is Natalie Wood, the movie star, and that must be her little girl Natasha who just happens to be the same age as my daughter Jessica!"

After the class let out, I went over to her and said, "Hi, are you Natalie? You're one of my all time favorites."

I made such a fool of myself that I am surprised she even talked to me. I introduced myself and pointed out my daughter who just happened to be the same age as her daughter, and she suggested that we get the little girls together sometime to play. I said that was a great idea. She wrote her number, name and address on a card and gave it to me. I was in shock. I was over the moon. I was so excited; not only had I met one of my movie star idols, but she had just invited me to come over to her house where she lived with her husband, Robert Wagner. I have kept that card until this very day.

Their house was very close to ours, only about a five-minute drive away. We made a plan for a play date for the girls, and she said to bring Aviva's swimming suit as they may go in the water. When I got there, the Russian grandma was taking care of Natasha and speaking to her in Russian. She seemed to be the caregiver, and Natalie was on a lawn chair with a big hat getting a little sun. She was friendly but elusive. While we would be in the middle of a conversation, she would hear "RJ" (as she called him) on the phone and she would yell out things like, "Ask him if he's an actor's director?" Then a few minutes later she would yell out, "Ask him if he's a director's director?"

They were very adoring with each other. It was as if they really "dug" each other. They were flirtatious, affectionate and jovial with one another. Meanwhile, the little girls seem to be ignoring each other. Maybe they were too young to play together yet.

About a month later, we were invited back to their house. Natalie was sitting on the steps of the pool with her feet in the water. She told me that she could not swim and she was afraid of the water. She also shared that she would never go in the deep end (in retrospect, how strange this was). RJ came to say goodbye, and she asked, "Where are you going?"

He said, "I got to go into town; I got a little honey there." He kissed her on the head and they both rather laughed. They were so cute together.

On my next visit, there was quite a lot of drama because there was a snake in the pool. Natalie was freaked out. One of the gardeners came and retrieved it, but nobody wanted to go near the water that day. Most of the visits we had with them were by the pool, and Aviva and Natasha barely talked to each other. I think the only people that Natasha had been around were adults, and mostly her grandmother. I think that is the reason that Natalie wanted to enroll her in nursery school. She wanted her to become more social and play with children her own age. I also think that is the only reason why she wanted me to come over with my daughter.

When it came time for Aviva's birthday, I invited Natalie and Natasha. They came and I think they had fun, but Natasha stuck very close to her mother. She did not want to play with the other kids. I took movies of the birthday party and I have Natalie in the background chewing on some ice. It was October 17 in Palm Springs, so it was still warm. Being that she was pregnant, she was trying to watch her weight and chewing on ice made her feel like she was eating something. Good trick, I thought to myself.

Aviva's father and I divorced after a few seasons in Palm Springs. I did not see Natalie again, until one day in Beverly Hills I saw her Rolls-Royce. I knew it was hers because her license plate read "NWW NWW". This meant that she had become Natalie Wood Wagner twice. I left her a little note on the windshield with my phone number but I never heard from her again.

Natalie wood died on November 28, 1981.

CHAPTER 24

My Roles In Television and Movies

Blackjack 1978

When I first came to Hollywood, I enrolled in an acting class immediately. I knew I had no experience on stage except for modeling, and that was a whole different ball of wax. When you were modeling on the ramp, all you cared about was what you looked like, your attitude, and remembering to hold in your stomach. That was it. You became a quick-change artist. You had to get in and out of your clothes as fast as you could and get into your next outfit. Then you would appear on the runway calm, as if you have been preparing the outfit all day. The runway was the show; in the back room was the chaos. It was so much fun. I would change clothes, shoes, jewelry and hats all in less than a minute. I loved the attention I got on the runway. I was one of the few models that smiled at the audience. Most of the models had their noses in the air and would act snotty, but I liked to smile and get the smiles back from the people watching the fashion show.

The only acting experience I had as child was at the lake in the summer. My older sister and I used to put on plays and invite people to come. We called them concerts and we had no idea what we were doing. It was all impromptu and usually a disaster. We would make tickets and give them out around the neighborhood to try to get people to come. We would then let them in free with their ticket. We never had much of an audience except maybe our grandparents and a few mothers and fathers. I was a little ham since I was a child. I used to sing and dance for the relatives, and they would give me quarters. I would make them laugh, too. That is what led to my stand up comedy career.

Back at the acting class, I met a new friend and fellow actor, Kurt. I think I had been in class with him for about six months when I got a call from Kurt saying he was in Las Vegas doing a movie called *Blackjack*. He told me that if I could get my ass to Las Vegas, he thought that they had a part for me. I quickly got my ass to Las Vegas. The director of the movie wrote a letter to Screen Actors Guild, saying that he needed an actress with a French look for this part, and therefore I got my SAG card. Woo hoo!

The part was less than spectacular. I played one of two hookers, and I think the only line I had was, "Do you know where I can plug this thing in?"

Hey, I was paid and I got my SAG card, so I was in actor's

heaven. (It is hard to work in Hollywood if you do not have a SAG card. In addition, you cannot get a SAG card without an agent but you cannot get an agent without a SAG card, so it is a catch-22.) I got my first movie with credits and my SAG card. I was on my way. I thought. I was going to be a big star. Ha ha.

Joe and Valerie

Joe and Valerie was a takeoff on *Saturday Night Fever.* It ran for two seasons and it was good. I originally heard about the series while it was in production, and that they were looking for background dancers. I knew I was an excellent dancer. I loved dancing so much; my mother had enrolled me in dance class when I was three-years-old. I later enrolled in The Royal Winnipeg Ballet's jazz classes. I was just crazy about dancing. I would go disco dancing with my best friend at least three nights a week. The most exclusive club was called Pips. I had a lawyer friend that used to put my name on the guest list so I could get in anytime I wanted. I was the disco queen. My plan was to go to the cattle call audition and dance my socks off and be noticed. Then they would ask me if I wanted a role in the series. (A cattle call is an audition where they invite as many as 300 people to audition all at the same time. They bring them in in groups, hence the name cattle call. We were all like cattle being herded in.) Well, intention is everything. I was noticed and they asked if I wanted a part in the series. Of course, I accepted with great excitement. In the part I would be dancing with one of the leads at a disco and doing an amazing choreographed dance number. My role could be compared to Donna Pescow's role n the original movie, *Saturday Night Fever*. I had lines as well, which was great because that made me eligible to get my American Federated Television and Radio Artists card. AFTRA was the union for television and radio performing artists, whereas SAG was for movies and commercial artists. Wow, my first year in Hollywood and I already had my SAG and my AFTRA cards. I thought I was definitely on the road to success in Hollywood.

Waverly Wonders 1978

JOE NAMATH

Between September and October 1978, I received a call from my agent that I had an audition for a new TV show called *Waverley Wonders*. The show was starring Joe Namath as a basketball coach. I was reading for the part of a flight attendant. There would be another actress cast as a flight attendant, and together we would be called "the dynamic duo." They cast a wonderful gorgeous actress, Suzi McIver. She had stunning red hair. We soon became close friends. Suzi was one of the original golden girls on the *Dean Martin Show*. She was an excellent dancer and an amazing actress. Suzi was married and I was single. Suzi and I were, indeed, the "dynamic duo." On the show, we were dating Joe Namath and his best friend Squire Frydel. I remember the scene very well; it was short and sweet and goofy. I was sitting on Squire's lap and we were all partying up a storm. The series never made it; after one season it was canceled. Joe Namath had asked for my phone number. He called and asked me to have dinner with him. I agreed. He picked me up at my residence in the slums of Beverly Hills. It was called the slums because it was the only area in Beverly Hills where you could rent an apartment at a reasonable price. It was on the outskirts of Beverly Hills. No mansions there, just apartment buildings and duplexes, but if you wanted your kids to go to good schools, you had to have the Beverly Hills zipcode. I suggested that we go to a restaurant that was nearby where some football players hung out, such as O.J. Simpson and his then girlfriend Nicole Simpson. Joe liked that idea and we proceeded to the restaurant. Joe was feeling somewhat out of sorts and said he thought he was coming down with a cold. I thought to myself, "Oh great, no kissing!"

When we arrived at the restaurant, it was very busy and the owner, whom I knew, said that there would be a 20-minute wait. What a big mistake! You do not make a big celebrity coming to your restaurant wait to be seated, you seat them immediately. Joe said, "Let's go." We left. We went to another restaurant, an Italian place on Santa Monica Blvd. It was quaint and they greeted him and treated him like the celebrity that he was. Immediately they sat us and bent over backwards to make sure that we had everything that we needed. I learned that Joe was a vegetarian. We had a pleasant dinner, but Joe was out of sorts! After dinner, he had his driver take him home to the Beverly Hills Hotel on Sunset Boulevard. He apologized to me for not feeling well and said we would talk soon. His driver brought me home. Although there were no major sparks between us, I thought possibly we would get together again. The events that took place after prevented that from ever happening. The next day, the owner of the restaurant where I had taken Joe called the *Hollywood Reporter* and gave them a scoop. The *Hollywood Reporter* ended up saying something like, "New hot couple in town, Joe Namath and Vicki Le Mere, slicing steak at Stellini's." What a huge lie! Not only did we not eat there, but also Joe was a vegetarian and did not eat meat. I called the owner, and asked, "Why did you say that when we didn't even eat there, you should have given him a table immediately."

He said, "Hey, I took advantage of the situation."

I was so disgusted with him, I never went there again.

As nice as it was to see my name in print in the *Holly-wood Reporter*, I would never betray someone's trust by doing something like that. When Joe Namath found out, he thought I set him up by taking him to my friend's restaurant. I had no such intention. I didn't even know where we were going to have dinner. I just suggested that place because I knew that some of the football players went there and I thought he would like that. We ended up, of course, going somewhere else. I did not know the idiot was going to call the *Hollywood Reporter* and give them a false scoop. C'est la vie!

That was the first time I had met Joe Namath. Fast forward twenty years or so, I had a friend visiting from Canada. He said he would like to see some movie stars, so I took him to the Polo Lounge at the Beverly Hills Hotel. Guess who was at the bar? Joe Namath. I said to my friend, "There is Joe Namath, I did a TV show with him."

He did not believe me, so I walked up to Joe and I said, "Hi Joe its Vicki, remember, we did *Waverley Wonders* together."

He said, "Vicki!" And gave me a big hug.

He did not realize I was with a date. As soon as I told him, we said our goodbyes. My friend was freaked out. He could not believe that I knew and had worked with Joe Namath. What a hoot for a Canadian boy. We also saw a couple of other stars that night. I think one of them was Frankie Avalon.

11th Victim

This was a movie made for television about The Hillside Strangler.

I auditioned for a part as one of the hookers (type cast again). I could not believe how hard the process was. First we went in front of the casting director, probably close to 300 women altogether. Then from that 300, they brought back six for callbacks. Those would go in front of the main producers and director. If you made it past that, you were one of three who got to go in front of the whole entourage of people involved in making this movie (producers, directors, etc.) There was a room full of approximately twenty people. I got this far, and when I walked into the room I felt nervous and naked. I had never read for that many people. It was very intimidating. It was the final stage before I got booked for the movie. I remember that I had dressed to look like a hooker. I had on a very short skirt and a very sexy top. Fortunately, at the time I had a hot body so I was quite confident in the way I looked. However, I was nervous about the auditioning side of it. Well, it went very well and I booked the part. The casting director was very pleased.

The movie had its premiere, and I brought a friend I was dating. I was in the opening scene of the movie. Unfortunately, I got whacked shortly after that so that was it. I was not in the rest of the movie. The friend I brought kept saying, "That is it? That is it?"

If he only knew how hard, I had worked to get that little part.

McLain's Law

This TV series aired in 1981-82. The star, James Arness, hoped to make a comeback after his long-time hit series *Gunsmoke.*

I got an audition for the show and nailed the part. It was

a very small part and the series only lasted for one season.

I think I could honestly say that I held the record for the most appearances in series that never made it past pilot season. (So much for becoming a big star in Hollywood.) I was never good at selling myself. I think I lacked the confidence to be bold. I really should have been a known working actress by now.

Erotic Images

The Playboy channel produced this TV series. I worked fourteen episodes, which I think was the most work that I have ever done as an actor. I played the part of an ex-Las Vegas showgirl married to a senator. The person they cast as the senator was a real asshole person I had met at a party a few months prior. I remember that there were four of us standing on the balcony in a house located off Laurel Canyon Boulevard. We were having a nice conversation, when I said something he did not like and he slapped my face. Other than being in a relationship with an abusive person, no stranger has ever slapped me and I have never slapped anyone. I was in shock and I just walked away. What was I going to do, slap him back and start a fistfight? The other girls standing there could not believe what he did. They said he was a real asshole, and I certainly agreed. You can understand my dismay when I got on the set and they told me that he was going to play the part of my husband.

When I read for the casting director, he told me there

would be tasteful nudity in two scenes that I would be shooting. I asked, "What do you mean by tasteful nudity?"

He replied, "Above the waist only."

This would be the first time I had done any kind nudity anywhere, so I was a little nervous about it. I had a bedroom scene, and the casting director had assured me that the only people on the set in that room would be people instrumental to that particular scene. Meaning the only people watching would be the director, the cinematographer, the lighting person, sound, etc. and any makeup or hair people as needed.

While waiting for my scene, I watched a few of the scenes that they were shooting and noticed that I was the only girl there that had real boobs. What a joke.

The storyline for this particular scene was that my husband was giving me some sort of a surprise for my birthday. He was pacing up and down and waiting for someone to come to the door. I was in bed, nude above the waist with the sheet pulled up over my boobs. As we got ready to shoot this particular scene, I looked around and lo and behold, the room was full. Not only was the casting director there, but everybody that was involved in the production wanted to get a look at this scene. I spoke to the director and told him that the room needed to be cleared of anyone who was not instrumental to this scene, as per my contract. He followed my request and cleared the room. I was not very confident in having myself naked from the waist up. We all know what happens to real breasts when we lie down. They go flat as a pancake. I was most anxious to get the scene over.

Back to the scene. There is a knock on the door, my husband rushes to open it and there stands a woman in a fur coat. She spoke with a Russian accent. Apparently, she was there to have a threesome with me and my husband. This was my surprise. As she approached the bed, she opened her coat. She was naked from the waist up. She leaned towards me to kiss me and I was hit with the worst body odor that I have ever experienced from a woman. Some surprise; it was more of a shock and I had to act interested in this woman. After kissing me, she started to move down my body under the sheets towards my pubic area, and the director called "cut."

I know the poor girl must have been standing out in the lights, with that horribly hot fur coat on, waiting until they had the scene ready to go. It can take an hour to set up one scene. Thank God, I did not have to expose my bare boobs for very long and that I was able to keep them under the sheets until we were ready to shoot.

Another scene that is stuck in my memory is a scene where we were all at a party and all of a sudden, for some reason, everybody started taking his or her clothes off. I remember I had on a one-piece gray silk jumpsuit. It had snaps down the front, so it was easy for me to just pull open the snaps and there they were, my boobs, the only real ones in the room. I was horrified. I was hoping the series would never air, but one of my Buddhist friends told me that he saw me on the Playboy channel. Yuck!

To this day, I have never seen this show, although now I am curious. Maybe I can look it up on YouTube.

Scarface

The year was 1983, and I had not done much since Erotic Images. My boyfriend at the time, Teddy, told me that his best friend Angel Salazar was working on an Al Pacino movie called *Scarface*. He was playing the part of Chi Chi, one of Al Pacino's right hand men. He said he might be able to get me in as a background artist, even though they had already cast everyone. He thought he could pull a few strings because of his connection. I went down to the set and they gave me SAG background artist status. What that means is I would make a little more money. When they needed an actress to focus the camera on, it would be one of seven SAG actors in the background.

I worked on the movie for two-and-a-half weeks. It was fun being around big stars; although they treated the background the artists like scum. Al Pacino would not make eye contact with any of the background artists. Many times I would be very close to him and look right at him, and he would look directly above my head so as never to make eye contact with me. Michelle Pfeiffer was a little friendlier. We had some conversations while we were waiting on the side to go in on the next scene. She talked to me and I asked her if she was normally so thin? She said she needed to lose weight for the part because she was portraying a woman with a drug problem. At least she talked to me. The story goes that she was a checker at Vons supermarket and someone discovered her and made her a star. What a story!

I was in all the scenes with large groups of people. The disco scenes, the restaurant scenes and all the performance scenes where there was someone on stage playing to a large audience. In one scene, there was a comedian on stage named Richard Belzer. He looked over at me sitting at a table with other women. The camera zoomed in on me and he said, "Hey is that Coke in your bra?"

I do not remember what the set up for that joke was; I just remember that it was my one of my big moments in the film. There was another scene when the clown was shot. He was coming up to my booth to ask me to dance when bullets started flying and everybody started scattering towards the exits. It took us hours to stage that scene so that everybody knew where he or she was crossing and which way he or she was going to which exits. They did not want us tripping and falling over each other (lawsuits). We were all scrambling, so it was close.

It was fun working on *Scarface*. I was really hoping that they would notice me and give me a line or two, but it never happened. There was a lot of hurry up and wait. If you have never worked on a big movie, you would not believe how tedious it is and how much has to be repeated over and over and over again. Actually making movies is very boring, even when you are starring in something. I remember one movie I did where I had my own trailer. I mostly sat there all day long with nothing to do. There was no internet in those days and no TV in our trailers. It was just me in my little trailer, and my name was on the outside. People would knock on the door and ask me for my autograph. Often they would say, "Who are you? Can I have your autograph?" La di da!

After working on *Scarface*, I started focusing more on my comedy and my one-woman show. I really liked doing both singing and comedy with a little acting and dance on the side. This combo fulfilled all the things I liked to do, as far as my performing in front of a live audience. During those years, I still did the odd acting jobs. In addition, I performed in some music videos. One was for an artist called D.R.A.M. I was in many scenes throughout this video. The next one I was in was for a female artist called Fray. I played a nosy neighbor looking out the window at all her trash in her yard.

I had a small part in the TV series called *Crossroads Café*. No big deal, nothing to write home about. Then I was in the TV series called *Missing "n" Time"* where I played a mother whose son was murdered. I worked a couple of days on that one, and it was good. This series was based on real stories that they were reenacting.

My one-woman show premiered at the Gardenia

Cabaret. I did two shows there and then took it on the road, so to speak. The owner of the club said I did a stellar performance. I was very happy.

CHAPTER 25

That's A Wrap—Covid Crash
Beauty Tips 24 &25

During Covid, I was unable to do any performing. I had a big comedy show booked at the Ice House on March 31, 2020. They were going to be filming it. This was a really big deal for me and possibly a chance to be seen by important people. The show was canceled due to Covid. I had another one woman show booked on March 15, 2020, and it was canceled at the last minute. The acting jobs dwindled to almost nothing.

I was happy to have my spiritual practice to keep my spirits up. I had to reinvent myself. I started exercising like a crazy person every day. I had worked my whole life since I was twelve-years-old. I was not going to fall apart or sit in front of the TV watching soap operas and eating bon bons.

In 2021, I did manage to book three different background artist jobs. In addition, most recently, I happily performed my one-woman show again and on October 31, Halloween 2021. It was great to be back on stage again and doing what I loved to do.

I hope you have enjoyed reading my book, as much as I have enjoyed writing it.

With that said, here are few final beauty tips:

Beauty Tip # 24—Be yourself. There is no other person like you in the whole world. You are a unique and wonderful person. Embrace your individuality and always love who you are from the inside out.

And finally...........the last beauty tip.

Beauty Tip # 25—Never lose hope. Keep your dreams alive. Dreams really do come true!

BEAUTY TIPS:

Beauty Tip #1—Use eye cream every night. Start whatever age you're at and never stop.

Beauty Tip #2—Never pull the skin around your eyes. You will break the elastic tissue that keeps the skin young. Once it's broken, it doesn't come back. Be careful with the skin all over your face but especially around the eyes.

Beauty Tip #3—Do facial exercises like men do when they are shaving. Pretend you are shaving without a blade. Also say the "A E I O Us." Exaggerate these vowels with extreme expressions on your face, out loud.

Beauty Tip # 4—Set intentions for yourself! I always intended to look a lot younger than my age as I got older.

Beauty Tip # 5—Never use soap on your face, it is drying and aging. Use cleansing cream and wash it off with a warm washcloth.

Beauty Tip # 6—Put on your face cream and eye cream while your face is still wet. This locks in the moisture and enhances the effects of your beauty treatment.

Beauty Tip #7—Do lip exercises. Hold the corners of your mouth and try to blow out and flap your lips, making a BRR-RR sound. Sort of the same way that horses do. It keeps the lips full and larger.

Beauty Tip # 8—Be Resilient! Roll with the punches. Take the lemons of life and make lemonade. A positive attitude is a beautiful thing and shows on your face.

Beauty Tip # 9—Exercise your spirit every day. Whatever your spiritual practice is does not matter; just make sure that you practice daily to maintain your happiness.

Beauty Tip # 10—Exercise your body and your mind every day. I play tennis and do yoga and Zumba, to name a few. To exercise my mind, I play word games where you have to come up with words on the timer. I also write, which is better exercise for the brain than reading. Exercising the body, the mind, and the spirit every day definitely shows on your face. These three elements are a necessary part of any beauty regiment

Beauty Tip # 11—Take responsibility for your own life and what has happened to you. This is one of the most powerful things I have learned and was a turning point in my life.

Beauty Tip # 12—Try to get at least seven hours of sleep a night. Sleeping is the time that your body rejuvenates, and your face as well.

Beauty Tip # 13- NEVER SLEEP ON YOUR FACE. Sleeping on your face causes wrinkles; nothing is more aging than sleeping on your face. I used to sleep on the side of my face, and one morning I woke up and I couldn't believe the lines that were pushed up around my eyes. I immediately forced myself to always sleep on my back, and if I find myself turning over, I wake myself up and I do not let myself sleep on my face. This is one of the reasons why I have looked ten to fifteeen years younger than my age throughout my life.

Beauty Tip # 14—SMILE! It is good for your face and good for your soul. I read somewhere in one of my many studies that it takes forty-seven muscles to smile and only seven to frown. So not only is it infectious when you smile, it also is good exercise for your face. Keep smiling and happiness will follow. When you smile, people smile back.

Beauty Tip # 15—As Winston Churchill said, "Never give up. Never ever ever!" Try to think positively about everything, because being negative only brings you negative results.

Beauty Tip number #16—Help other people who are suffering. It will help lessen your own suffering and make you more beautiful.

Beauty Tip # 17—Do not pluck your eyebrows too thin, or remove them all together and draw a fake line. Nothing ages you more than that look. If you have no eyebrows, have them tattooed in tiny brush strokes or draw them in, that way.

Beauty Tip# 18—Stop wearing eye shadow when you get older, it makes you look older, especially the glitter kind. If you are going to wear eye shadow over fifty, wear a neutral matte color.

Beauty Tip # 19—Do not drink too much. Getting drunk and having hangovers will age you dramatically.

Beauty Tip # 20—DO NOT SMOKE! Next to the sun, it has the most aging effect on the face. If you do not want to stop for your health, which is a damn good reason, at least stop for your looks, your beauty. SAVE YOUR FACE.

Beauty Tip # 21—Do not let anyone take away your happiness. Do not stay in an abusive or unsatisfactory relationship. Life is too short for that!

Beauty Tip # 22—Love yourself. Until you do, no one else will. Develop self love. Affirmations, acts of kindness to yourself. For example, get a massage.

Beauty Tip # 23—Keep your sense of humor about everything. Learn to laugh at yourself and see the humor in your disasters.

Beauty Tip # 24—Be yourself. There is no other person like you in the whole world. You are a unique and wonderful person. Embrace your individuality and always love who you are from the inside out.

Beauty Tip # 25—Never lose hope. Keep your dreams alive. Dreams really do come true!

Photo References

In reference to the photos that are in the center of book:

Page 1—Through the years ages 1 through 9
  Picture one—"me and my favorite doll."

  Picture two—"Flowers flowers. I am a flower model."

  Picture three—"yep, it's just me and my boyfriend."

  Picture four—"Hello, I can't hear you?"

  Picture five—"When's the prom?"

  Picture six—"woo hoo, ride-'em cowgirl."

Page 2—Through the years ages 15 to 30
  Picture one—age 15, what's up with pointed bras?

  Picture two, three and four - modeling for a coat manufacture

  Picture five—first summer in California at the beach in Marina Del Rey

  Picture six—first and second professional head shots

Page 3—Air Force pinup model
  Air Force pinup girl for the Canadian Air Force

Page 4—Newspaper model ads
  1970s newspaper ads for the Hudson Bay Company and Eaton's, the two largest Department stores in Canada at the time.

Page 5—Le Mere Jewelry
  Le Mere jewelry through the years. My store on Melrose Avenue

Page 6—Entertainment—Singing, Comedy
  One Women Shows, Performances at: The Gardenia, Gazzaries, The Ha Ha Comedy club, The Comedy Store, and The Improv

Page 7—my family (Todd, my son) and granddaughters
Picture one—Me and Brian at the lake. Nicky and Todd's father

Picture two—Me and my son Todd at one of my birthdays

Picture three—Me and my baby girl Aviva doing puzzles

Picture four—Me and my three children

Picture five—me and my granddaughters and my great granddaughters

Page 8—my family (Nicky, my daughter) And the Boys
Picture one—Nicky, my daughter, Finley, my grandson hiding, Bodhi, my grandson, and Ronnie, my son-in-law

Picture two—Me and my grandsons. Finley, flower the dog, grandma, Bodhi—the rockstar

Page 9—4 decades
Picture one—40s

Picture two—50 birthday

Picture three—60th birthday

Picture four—70th birthday

Page 10—Memorandum

With light, love and remembrance
Picture one—me and Marcel. One picture taken in 1999 and the other one, twenty years later in 2019.

Picture two—my dearest sweetest best friend ever, Joyce. Miss you more than words can express.

Picture three—my dear Lawyer friend Danny. We dated when I was in my twenties and we remained friends till the day he passed.

Picture four—Kiki. A dynamite feisty lady for her little size. One of the girls group, a great cook and we had many laughs together

Picture five—Bridget, one of my dearest friends for thirty-five years. Her life was cut way too short. Brought her into the girls group. We laughed and partied our asses off.

Acknowledgments

It took so many people besides myself, to write this book I certainly couldn't have done it without the help of my amazing coach, Mary Lou Reid. Her kind and gentle prodding got me through many discouraging moments.

The pictures in the middle wouldn't have not come to life and been displayed so beautifully, without the artistic eye of my dear friend and graphic artist Jeff Oliver. Many thanks for the many hours you put into this and your heart and soul.

The beautiful design of the cover and the interior were put together by the amazing Christy Day. She's a true artist and a wonderful person. Working with her was a gift.

I would be remiss if I didn't mention my dear best friend, Pamela de Almeida. She's been there to support me, physically, mentally, and emotionally. Thank you Pam. Friends like you are hard to find.

About the Author

VICKI LE MERE is the author of *Saving Face*. Vicki believes that all women can look and feel great as they age without the need for plastic surgery. In this book, the author shares the many secrets of her lifelong journey of struggles and triumphs, and the keys she learned to finding true happiness, peace and beauty from the inside out. Vicki was born Prince Rupert, British Columbia and raised in Winnipeg, Manitoba, Canada, where she worked as a model from age fifteen to thirty. She left Canada and came to Hollywood to pursue an acting career. She has appeared on stage, screen and television and has been doing stand-up comedy for over twenty years. She has owned her own costume jewelry business for thirty-five years. Vicki enjoys playing tennis, practicing yoga, hiking and Zumba. She became a Buddhist at thirty-eight and found the key to true happiness through her own inner transformation. She is a Buddhist leader in her community, and works diligently for world peace through individual happiness. She has helped countless individuals overcome their suffering. Vicki knows that all people have the potential to become absolutely happy. Vicki is a mother of three, a grandmother of four, and a great grandmother of three. Her children are her greatest joy.